Leemei Tan

Lemongrass
and
Ginger

vibrant asian recipes

DUNCAN BAIRD PUBLISHERS

LONDON

DEDICATION
This book is dedicated to my family,
Arnaud, Nelly, Azma and Kristin.

First published in the United Kingdom and Ireland in 2012 by Duncan Baird Publishers Ltd
Sixth Floor, Castle House, 75–76 Wells Street
London W1T 3QH

Conceived, created and designed by Duncan Baird Publishers

Managing Editor: Grace Cheetham
Editors: Camilla Davis and Josephine Bonde
Art Director and Designer: Manisha Patel
Production: Uzma Taj
Commissioned Photography: Yuki Sugiura
Food Stylist: Aya Nishimura
Prop Stylist: Wei Tang

British Library Cataloguing-in-Publication Data:
A CIP record for this book is available from the British Library

ISBN: 978-1-84899-007-4

10 9 8 7 6 5 4 3 2 1

Typeset in Arno Pro and Questal
Colour reproduction by Colourscan, Singapore
Printed in China by Imago

PUBLISHER'S NOTE:
While every care has been taken in compiling the recipes for this book, Duncan Baird Publishers, or any other persons who have been involved in working on this publication, cannot accept responsibility for any errors or omissions, inadvertent or not, that may be found in the recipes or text, nor for any problems that may arise as a result of preparing one of these recipes. It is important that you consult a medical professional before following any of the recipes or information contained in this book if you have any special dietary requirements or medical conditions. Ill or elderly people, babies, young children and women who are pregnant or breastfeeding should avoid recipes containing raw meat, raw fish or uncooked eggs.

NOTES ON THE RECIPES:
Unless otherwise stated:
• All recipes serve 4
• Use medium eggs, fruit and vegetables
• Use fresh ingredients, including herbs and chillies
• Do not mix metric and imperial measurements
• 1 tsp = 5ml   1 tbsp = 15ml   1 cup = 250 ml

contents

INTRODUCTION

Home for me is Kedah in the northwestern state of Peninsula Malaysia where I grew up with my mum, dad, big sister and little brother. Picturesque, complete with lush paddy fields and dotted with kampungs (villages), the Kedah region is the 'Rice Bowl of Malaysia', producing more than half of Malaysia's rice supply.

Malaysia is a society where many diverse food cultures mix so, as I grew up, not only did I have the opportunity to eat many different foods but also I was encouraged by my parents to be bold and adventurous with what I ate. Delicious foods of all kinds were available to us in abundance, and right on our doorstep.

I grew up in a town where the main street was lined on both sides with a collection of shops and homes, and this is where we lived. Dad ran his retail business downstairs, we lived upstairs, and in our large backyard my mum grew chilli bushes, pandan plants and mango, papaya and calamansi (a type of citrus fruit) trees. We also raised free-range chickens.

Serving fresh, healthy and scrumptious meals to her family was important to my Mum, and each day after we left for school she would make her way to the nearby markets to source the freshest ingredients to use when cooking our dinner. Because Friday was the first day of the weekend in Kedah State it meant I could join Mum at the markets. After what seemed like years of nagging her to let me come along, my first outing to the markets was a real adventure. One hand clinging onto my small straw bag and the other holding onto Mum's hand, I was mesmerized by the sounds, sights and smells. Traders and farmers vying for each customer's business; displays of amazing fresh fruits and vegetables; and massive boxes of crushed ice covering fresh seafood and fish shipped in daily from the two main shipping ports – Kuala Perlis and Kuala Kedah. I found it captivating, but equally as exciting for me was watching Mum turn all the wonderful fresh produce into amazing food. It was never a chore for me to get involved in the kitchen; I was a willing volunteer, taking on any task Mum felt confident I could cope with.

MUM'S LITTLE HELPER

Those early years in the kitchen – learning about different fresh roots, spices and other important ingredients in an Asian kitchen; helping with the chopping, grinding, pounding and slicing; and observing my mum gutting fish and preparing fresh poultry before cooking – are all experiences that have definitely formed my appreciation of fresh produce and my love of creating new dishes. Food was such an important part of my upbringing, and it wasn't until quite a few years later that I understood just how priceless this time was. Even though I was a very willing helper, there were times when I moaned about how the chores given to me were all related to food preparation: 'Why can't I cook a dish?', I would ask. The response was always the same, 'You have plenty to learn before I let you handle the wok.' I would pull a long and sulky face, not realizing that Mum wanted me to have a solid base in cooking. Back then, I could only observe how to do proper stir-frying, braising and steaming, but now I realize just how clever and insightful Mum was.

MY FORMATIVE YEARS

After I finished high school, I went to a college in Kuala Lumpur, and during this time, eating out became part of my lifestyle. There were street food hawkers almost at every corner, and it didn't take me long to get enthusiastic about the food scene. Along with eating street food, I used to eat regularly at restaurants, so I got to experience many different cuisines from around the world, further fueling my interest in food. But there is something quite special about home-cooking, and I had always been pampered with Mum's. Luckily for me I had a wonderful landlady who was both kind and a very good cook. Mrs Seow often spoiled me with her home cooking. I will always remember fondly how on hot, humid days she would treat me to a traditional soupy dessert to help cool me down. Another lip-smacking, simple yet flavoursome dish that she prepared was Claypot Chicken Rice (*see page 88*). Her secret was to use a free-range chicken and to be bold with seasoning.

From Kuala Lumpur I moved to Perth, Australia, for two years to complete my university degree. Leaving my home and my family was very hard, but I was embarking on a new adventure and I was with a group of friends. This period of my life turned out to be one of those important milestones in my life – it was also where my cooking skills were put to the test.

I shared a house with three friends: Peh-Ling, who was not confident in her cooking skills, so she was in charge of chopping the vegetables; Huey-Mein, who cooked a little, but everything looked dark and tasted sweet, as she is very fond of dark and sweet soy sauce; and there was Cathy, who like me had had a lot more hands-on experience in the kitchen. It was Cathy and I who ended up cooking most of the time.

As in my parents' house, we would always sit down to a bowl of fluffy white rice, which we would eat with a few different meat, fish and vegetable dishes, all nicely presented at the centre of the table – fresh and simple; fragrant and warm; delicious and healthy. I have many fond memories of this time, and quite recently Cathy and I were reminiscing about our mealtime moments when she suddenly paused and exclaimed, 'Never once did it cross anyone's mind to start dinner without everyone being home!' And it was our home away from home, a house filled with warmth and laughter. During those few years, cooking without any guidance from Mum, I learned to improvise, and this made me a keener and more confident cook.

LIVING IN LONDON

From Perth I returned to Kuala Lumpur to work, then, about seven years ago, I decided to take a sabbatical and pursued my dream to travel and experience more of the amazing world we live in. I headed for London, where I'm still based. My first year in London flew by. I cooked more than I used to back in Malaysia, and my weekly telephone conversations with Mum were never without a discussion of food of some kind. There was also lots of 'How do you … ?', 'Do you remember that dish that you made … ?' and 'You know the

spice paste that was freshly ground, how much of each ingredient do I use?'
It was during this year that I realized just how much I had taken for granted
during the cooking sessions in my parents' kitchen, and just how infectious
Mum's enthusiasm had been!

It was during my second year in London, after I met my now fiancé,
Arnaud, that the next stage of my food journey started. Along with our
shared passion for food, we both love travelling, and Arnaud being French,
meant we made many trips to France. Slowly I was introduced to a different
style of cooking from the many different regions of France, and new and
amazing ingredients that were so different from those we use in Malaysia.

Arnaud's mother, Nelly, also loves cooking and enjoys good food,
and for her, as it is for me cooking is relaxing, therapeutic and never a chore.
When I first met Nelly, I didn't speak French or she Mandarin or English, and
it was food that helped us to connect with each other. Nelly, like my mum, is
one of the best role models. Her impeccable skills inspire me, and I love her
home cooking. It was meeting Arnaud and then Nelly that got me wondering,
'Is working with food my destiny?'

Travelling with Arnaud to the different regions in France and to many
different countries, experiencing the wonderful diversity of culture and styles
of cooking, has greatly influenced my own cooking. From each place I visit, I
come away with a handful of recipes and a new appreciation of what authentic
cooking means, inspiring me to learn new cooking techniques and to develop
my cooking style with an increasingly more international and modern flavour.

One life-changing experience was my visit to Tsukiji fish market in
Tokyo, which gave me an insight into the importance of eating top-quality
and fresh ingredients and preparing food simply. When you cook with fresh
produce, you can turn a good dish into something that is exceptionally tasty,
even when using the simplest cooking techniques. Nothing is more amazing
than eating the freshest tuna sashimi, sliced in a particular way, which
practically melts in your mouth. Even eating a freshly-made bowl of the

humble soba noodles, can bring about beaming, satisfied faces. At Tsujiki fish market, and generally when travelling through Japan, I learnt so much about the importance of the words 'practical, simple, healthy and delicious' when it comes to cooking and food, and this is now central to my style of cooking – and a great example of this is my Soy & Mirin Tuna on Soba Noodles (*see page 30*).

Simplicity lets the food speak for itself. If ever asked what is the most memorable dish I ate when travelling somewhere specific, my answer seems always to be something that was prepared in home-cooking style – simply presented yet bursting with flavour. And when I get home and recreate these dishes in my own kitchen, I get great satisfaction from this approach.

I remember a particular experience when I was in Vietnam that instilled in me, and reassured me, that in the kitchen patience is a virtue. (And now I pay even more attention to how soup stock tastes and looks.) I watched an amazing lady in her 60s start her day at 4am to prepare the stock for her version of Vietnamese Chicken Noodle Soup (*see page 144*) that she later sold on her food stall. Onions and ginger were toasted until slightly charred before adding them to the water – along with star anise, cinnamon sticks, cloves and chicken carcasses – to make a fresh, rich stock. Over the lowest heat possible, she left the ingredients to simmer ever so gently for hours, so as to avoid any cloudiness. The result was the most delicious, deep and flavoursome stock – with a hint of liquorice, cloves, onions and ginger. That, for me, is the result of patience and passion in cooking, which then brings warmth and happiness to those people who get to enjoy the meal.

Travelling has given me the incredible opportunity to immerse myself in learning about local foods and a country's culture. And I have had many fantastic and special experiences, when I have spent time really talking with local people to understand their culture, which, especially in Asian countries, has often evolved through food and, in particular, spice trading.

These conversations and observations have made me realize just how important, if not essential, it is to preserve the authenticity of recipes however much you adapt and modernize them. And this realization was in part the impetus behind starting my food and travel blog, My Cooking Hut, in 2007. I wanted to do my bit to spread the love of food, and its heritage, to other people all around the world.

MY COOKING HUT

For me, my blog is not only a way to record my food and travel experiences, but also a way to share and reminisce with fellow food and travel enthusiasts. Food is a wonderful way to bond people together, and through the world of blogging I have connected with so many fantastic, like-minded people from many different cultures and parts of the world.

It may only be a small contribution, but I hope that sharing my passion, knowledge and skills will inspire an interest in food and the origin of different dishes in people of all ages, and help them to appreciate just how closely related food and the lifestyles we live are.

Stepping into the food blogging world may not have been planned, but it has given me a better insight into many different cuisines and it has allowed me to explore my own talents and interests. It was through writing and talking about food that led me to food photography and styling. Never before had I appreciated the potential I showed in these areas, and as each day passes and I further submerge myself in my blog work my passion grows stronger. Photography has enabled me to look at things differently and capture not only the beauty of food but to appreciate some of the amazing scenery that God has blessed our world with.

What keeps me going is the encouragement that I receive from the loyal readers of my blog. Every day I am touched by the sweet and kind words I receive. I am so thankful for them, and it is this appreciation that makes me even more determined to produce and share beautiful recipes and photography.

LEMONGRASS & GINGER

Writing the recipes for this book, remembering all the people and places that have inspired me and reflecting on just how far my food journey has taken me since that first trip to the market with Mum, has been, if truth be told, almost unbelievable. As I've sat in front of my computer screen typing away, so many vivid images have popped back into my mind that I can almost smell and taste the food, hear the banter and laughter, and feel the joy of sharing these moments with friends, family and new-found, food-loving enthusiasts. Being able to bring these experiences to life in my kitchen, and now in this book for you to cook and enjoy, is incredibly rewarding; to have this opportunity to show you just how tasty, rich and flavoursome authentic Asian cooking is – and how easy it is to prepare at home.

The recipes in this book are my take on wonderful, classic recipes of Southeast Asia. Many of them use modern ingredients and equipment – and different, more approachable techniques. They include recipes for dishes I have tasted during my travels that stand out in my memory. There are some that have been handed down from my family and others that are recipes that were inspired by meals I enjoyed with people I've met or have eaten with family and friends.

As you flip through the book and read the recipes, you will discover, as I have, the significant differences in dishes from one country to the next, despite the countries bordering one another, such as China and India; or, even though two countries are far apart, incredible similarities between the ingredients and spices, as in Malaysian and Indian cuisines. There are so many different types of delicious Asian foods with amazing flavours and wonderful ranges of tastes, and the recipes I've included within each chapter have been chosen specifically so you can experience the diversity of Asian food.

When writing and compiling the recipes, it was important to me that they accurately reflect the flavours and nuances of the different countries, and to do this, a lot of fresh spices are used. Within the Basics section of the book you will find 20 spice pastes (*see pages 206–210*) that are so easy to make, you will never again need to buy the ready-made versions. Using either a food processor or mortar and pestle, you can grind up fresh spice pastes in just a few minutes. Each paste recipe makes enough for one recipe or a meal for four people, but can easily be doubled, tripled, etc., and can also be stored in the fridge for up to one week.

No matter which Asian cuisine you are cooking, the balance of flavours is very important. There is no secret to making the most perfect and tastiest dish – it all lies in the tasting and balancing of flavours. So, when cooking my recipes, or if you are taking inspiration from them to create your own, taste, taste and taste again while you are cooking. This is an important Asian cooking technique that I guarantee will help you to achieve a harmony of flavours in every dish you cook.

Another important tip, as mentioned before, is to use the freshest ingredients possible. And if you have a well-stocked storecupboard, with all the condiments essential to Asian cooking, such as light soy sauce, dark soy sauce, sweet soy sauce, fish sauce, Chinese rice wine, cooking sake, mirin and sesame oil, you can create healthy and tasty Asian food at home with ease.

I live to eat, and love to eat, and I know this will never change. I hope when you are reading and using my book you will be inspired and I manage to set off a similar passion for good, fresh food.

JAPAN & Korea

In contrast to the spiciness of Korean and other Asian foods, Japanese cuisine is mild in flavour with sweetness and saltiness as the key tastes. It is simple, light and elegant, and is cooked using the best-quality and freshest ingredients available. In Japanese cooking, there is an emphasis on the purity of the natural ingredient and eating seasonally. Key ingredients used are shoyu, Japanese soy sauce; mirin, a sweetened sake; rice wine vinegar; and miso, a fermented bean paste, which is also an ingredient used to make Japanese stock. Rice is also an important part of Japanese meals, and is the base ingredient of many favourite dishes, including Sea Bream Nigirizushi (*see page 25*) and Tempura Prawn Temaki (*see page 29*).

Korean food is largely rice- and noodle-based, and because of the liberal use of Korean hot red chilli pepper and hot pepper paste is very much associated with piquancy. Other key ingredients used in Korean cooking are soy sauce, garlic, ginger, spring onions, sesame oil and toasted sesame seeds, and nearly all meals are served with Kimchi, a Korean pickle most commonly made with cabbage (the use of Pak Choi (*see page 36*) is my tweak on the classic). There is an abundance of seafood in Korean cooking and pork and chicken are often eaten, but beef is by far the most popular meat, which is used in dishes such as Bibimbap (*see page 22*) and Sesame Barbecued Beef (*see page 24*).

cHICKen TerIYAKI & OnIgIrI Bento

Delicious, healthy and convenient is how I describe a bento. A simple packed lunch that consists of vegetables, meat or fish and rice. There are many variations of bento, and you can include anything you like – not just what I've selected here.

SERVES 4
PREPARATION TIME 25 minutes, plus 25 minutes marinating time
COOKING TIME 15–20 minutes, plus cooking the rice

150ml/5fl oz/scant ⅔ cup mirin
100ml/3½fl oz/generous ⅓ cup shoyu
2 tbsp sake
2 tbsp granulated sugar
1cm/½in piece of root ginger, peeled and finely grated, pulp discarded, reserving the juice
4 chicken legs, skin on and deboned (*see page 215*)
1 tbsp sesame seeds
½ recipe quantity Boiled Short-Grain Rice (*see page 214*)
400g/14oz baby leaf spinach
1 tbsp sunflower oil
250g/9oz cherry tomatoes
sea salt

1 Put the mirin, shoyu, sake, sugar and ginger juice in a bowl. Mix until the sugar is dissolved, then add the chicken legs and coat well in the liquid. Cover with cling film and leave to marinate in the fridge for about 25 minutes.

2 Meanwhile, heat a frying pan over a medium-high heat, then add the sesame seeds and dry-fry for a few minutes until the seeds begin to pop. Tip onto a plate and leave to one side.

3 Divide the warm, boiled rice into 8 equal portions. Moisten your hands to stop the rice sticking to them and scoop up a portion of rice. Shape it into a ball, then slightly flatten and sprinkle over the toasted sesame seeds. Repeat with the remaining portions of rice and leave to one side.

4 Bring a saucepan of salted water to the boil, add the spinach and cook for about 30 seconds. Drain and refresh the spinach under running cold water. Squeeze out any excess liquid and pat dry with kitchen paper. Divide into 4 equal portions, then shape each portion into 3 small balls. Leave to one side.

5 Heat the oil in a large saucepan over a medium-high heat. Add the chicken pieces, skin-side down, and cook for 5–6 minutes on each side until golden brown and the chicken is cooked through. Pour in the marinade and bring to the boil for a few seconds, then reduce the heat to medium and continue to cook the chicken until the sauce starts to thicken.

6 Remove from the heat and cut the chicken into bite-sized slices. To assemble, divide the rice portions, spinach balls, chicken and cherry tomatoes into each bento or lunch box.

korean Fried chicken

A few years ago in New York, I stopped by a popular Korean eatery that is most famous for one dish – Double-fried Chicken. That doesn't sound so sensational, right? I took my first bite from the chicken wing and was left speechless. Really crispy skin glazed with a soy sauce mixture. Amazing! I just wanted to keep eating and eating. Here I've recreated the recipe with the addition of sesame seeds for extra crunch.

SERVES 4
PREPARATION TIME 20 minutes
COOKING TIME about 1 hour

100g/3½oz/heaped ¾ cup
   plain flour, plus extra for
   dusting
3 tbsp cornflour
4 tbsp light soy sauce
1 tbsp granulated sugar
2 tbsp honey
1 tbsp sesame oil
4 garlic cloves, finely chopped
1cm/½in piece of root ginger,
   peeled and finely chopped
2 tbsp sesame seeds
500ml/17fl oz/2 cups
   sunflower oil, for deep-frying
1kg/2lb 4oz chicken wings

TO SERVE
1 recipe quantity Boiled
   Long-Grain Rice (*see page
   214*)

1 Sieve the plain flour and cornflour into a bowl, then gradually mix in 200ml/7fl oz/scant 1 cup water to form a batter and leave to one side.

2 In a small saucepan over a medium-high heat, add the soy sauce, sugar, honey, sesame oil, garlic, ginger and 1 tablespoon water. Bring to a gentle boil, then reduce the heat to low and simmer for 10 minutes until the mixture starts to thicken. Remove from the heat, strain over a large bowl and leave to one side.

3 Meanwhile, heat a frying pan over a medium-high heat, then add the sesame seeds and dry-fry for a few minutes until the seeds begin to pop. Tip onto a plate and leave to one side.

4 Heat the sunflower oil in a deep, heavy-based saucepan to 180°C/350°F or until a small piece of bread turns brown in 15 seconds. Lightly dust the chicken wings with flour, then coat with the batter and gently slide into the oil. Fry the wings in 2 or 3 batches for 10–15 minutes per batch until lightly golden brown, then remove from the oil, using a slotted spoon, and drain on kitchen paper. Avoid overcrowding the saucepan, as this will lower the temperature of the oil.

5 Let the chicken wings cool for 5 minutes and bring the heat back to 180°C/350°F. Re-fry the chicken in batches for a further 2 minutes per batch, or until golden brown and crisp, then remove from the oil and drain well on kitchen paper. Put the chicken pieces in the large bowl with the soy sauce mixture and toss until well coated. Sprinkle over the toasted sesame seeds and serve warm with boiled rice.

Japanese Pork & Cabbage Pancakes

Osaka in Japan is a heaven for food lovers, and when you stroll around its recognized area of gastronomy, Dotonburi, you are spoilt for choice. Restaurants line both sides of the streets. One of the specialities from Osaka is Okonomiyaki, a savoury pancake cooked on a griddle and topped with a Worcestershire-like sauce, mayonnaise and bonito. It is also very popular in the area of Hiroshima, but instead of mixing all the ingredients into the batter, Hiroshima-style Okonomiyaki, Bibimbap, is prepared by layering the ingredients.

MAKES 8 pancakes
PREPARATION TIME 25 minutes
COOKING TIME about 1 hour
  20 minutes

220g/7¾oz/heaped 1¾ cups
  plain flour
½ tsp sea salt
1 tbsp sake
1 tbsp mirin
½ small white cabbage, core
  removed, rinsed and finely
  chopped
150g/5½oz pork mince
150g/5½oz raw, peeled large
  king prawns, deveined and
  cut into small pieces (*see
  page 216*)
2 spring onions, finely
  chopped
2 eggs, at room temperature
sunflower oil, for oiling
light mayonnaise, to serve
bonito flakes, to serve
  (optional)

SAUCE
3 tbsp tomato ketchup
4 tbsp Worcestershire sauce
2 tsp golden syrup
2 tsp shoyu

1 To make the sauce, put the tomato ketchup, Worcestershire sauce, golden syrup and shoyu in a small saucepan over a medium-high heat. Stir well and cook for 2–3 minutes until the sauce starts to thicken. Leave to one side to cool.

2 Sift the flour into a large mixing bowl, add 230ml/7¾fl oz/scant 1 cup water and mix well to form a thick batter. Stir in the salt, sake and mirin, then add the cabbage, pork, prawns and spring onions. Break in the eggs, mix until well combined and set aside.

3 Pour some oil into a large, heavy-based frying pan over a medium-high heat, then use kitchen paper to grease the pan evenly and soak up any excess oil. When the pan is hot, add 3–4 tablespoons of the mixture and flatten it into a 12cm/4½in disc. Cook for 8–10 minutes, then, using a spatula, flip over the okonomiyaki and cook the other side for 8–10 minutes until golden brown and crisp. Remove from the pan and keep warm while you make the remaining pancakes. If they will fit in the pan, cook 2 okonomiyaki at a time. Oil the pan again, as required.

4 Divide the okonomiyaki between individual serving plates, brush with the sauce and then top with a generous dollop of mayonnaise and a scattering of bonito flakes, if using. Serve hot.

Japanese Beef Stew

The Japanese absolutely love to eat beef cooked in hotpot-style such as Nikujaga. The beef is very thinly sliced, stir-fried and then simmered with vegetables in a flavourful dashi. Here I suggest using beef topside or rump; however, for a truly sensational dish you could use wagyu beef. Originating in Japan, wagyu is now available worldwide. The fat is evenly distributed throughout the flesh and melts as the meat is cooked, giving it a soft and juicy texture and a rich flavour.

SERVES 4–6
PREPARATION TIME 20 minutes, plus making the Dashi
COOKING TIME 45 minutes

80g/2¾oz sugar snap peas
1 tbsp sunflower oil
500g/1lb 2oz casserole steak, trimmed of fat and cut into bite-sized pieces
1 onion, cut into wedges
3 carrots, cut into bite-sized pieces
2 potatoes, quartered
1 parsnip, cut into bite-sized pieces
250g/9oz daikon, quartered
½ recipe quantity Dashi (*see page 211*)
2 tbsp sake or rice wine
2 tbsp sugar
4 tbsp shoyu

TO SERVE
1 recipe quantity Boiled Long-Grain Rice (*see page 214*)

1 Prepare a bowl of ice-cold water and bring a saucepan of water to the boil. Add the sugar snap peas to the boiling water and blanch for 1–2 minutes. Drain, then put the sugar snaps into the iced water to stop the cooking process. Leave to one side.

2 Heat the oil in a frying pan or saucepan over a medium-high heat. Add the beef and cook, stirring occasionally, for 3 minutes until sealed and beginning to brown. Add the onion and cook for 2–3 minutes until soft and translucent, then add the carrots and cook for 3 minutes, or until almost tender.

3 Tip in the potatoes, parsnip, daikon, dashi, sake and sugar. Bring to the boil and then push the ingredients around the pan, making sure the vegetables are covered by the dashi. Reduce the heat to low, cover and simmer for 20 minutes. Add the shoyu and prepared sugar snap peas and cook, covered, for a further 5 minutes. Serve immediately with boiled rice.

BIBIMBAP

'Bibim' in Korean means to mix and 'bap' means rice, so this dish literally means 'mixed rice'. There is a popular variation of Bibimbap – Dol Sot Bibimbap – where the cooked rice is spread over the base of a stone pot and becomes crunchy during cooking. The other cooked ingredients are arranged on the rice and then a raw egg is added just before serving and stirred into the rice to cook it.

SERVES 4
PREPARATION TIME 30 minutes, plus 25 minutes freezing and soaking time
COOKING TIME 45 minutes

200g/7oz beef fillet, wrapped and semi-frozen for 25 minutes (*see page 217*)
2 tbsp sunflower oil
1 garlic clove, finely chopped
1 tbsp light soy sauce
6 dried shiitake mushrooms, soaked, drained and cut into thin strips (*see page 217*)
1 tsp sesame oil
120g/4¼oz/generous 1 cup bean sprouts
1 small carrot, cut into matchsticks
1 courgette, thinly sliced
200g/7oz baby leaf spinach
4 eggs
1 recipe quantity Boiled Short-Grain Rice (*see page 214*)
freshly ground black pepper

TO SERVE
1 tbsp sesame seeds
Korean hot pepper paste

1 Heat a frying pan over a medium-high heat, then add the sesame seeds and dry-fry for a few minutes until the seeds begin to pop. Tip onto a plate and leave to one side.

2 Remove the partially frozen beef from the freezer and unwrap the cling film. Using a sharp knife, cut the beef against the grain into 3mm/⅛in-thick slices.

3 Heat 1 tablespoon of the sunflower oil in a frying pan over a medium-high heat. Add the garlic and stir-fry for 1 minute, then add the beef and stir-fry for 5–6 minutes until brown and cooked through. Add the soy sauce and season with pepper. Remove the beef from the pan and keep warm. Still over a medium-high heat, add the shiitake mushrooms to the pan and stir-fry for 2 minutes, then drizzle over the sesame oil. Remove the mushrooms from the pan, using a slotted spoon, leave to one side and keep warm. Repeat the same process, without adding the sesame oil, with the bean sprouts and then the carrot.

4 Meanwhile, steam the courgette for 5 minutes, or until soft, and leave to one side. Steam the spinach for 2–3 minutes until wilted, then drain, squeeze out any excess water and leave to one side.

5 Heat the remaining sunflower oil in a large frying pan over a medium heat and fry the eggs for about 3 minutes each – the yolks should still be runny. Meanwhile, gently warm the beef and vegetables in a separate frying pan.

6 To assemble, divide the warm cooked rice into serving bowls, then divide the beef and vegetables between the dishes. Put a fried egg in the centre of each bowl. Sprinkle over the sesame seeds and serve immediately with the Korean hot pepper paste on the side.

sesame barbecued beef

Bulgogi is one of two dishes (*see* Pak Choi Kimchi *on page 36 for the other*) that really stuck with me after my first visit to Korea. The beef was very thinly sliced and gently marinated, then served raw on a platter with vegetables for each guest to cook on a shared grill at the table. Keeping the delicious, clean flavours, here is a modern take on the traditional dish with everything cooked in a pan instead.

SERVES 4
PREPARATION TIME 15 minutes, plus 1 hour 25 minutes freezing and marinating time
COOKING TIME 20 minutes

500g/1lb 2oz rib-eye steak or sirloin, wrapped and semi-frozen for 25 minutes (*see page 217*)
3½ tbsp light soy sauce
2 tbsp granulated sugar
2 tbsp sesame oil
3 garlic cloves, finely chopped
1cm/½in piece of root ginger, peeled and finely chopped
1 onion, sliced
2 tbsp sesame seeds
1 tbsp sunflower oil
2 spring onions, finely chopped

TO SERVE
1 recipe quantity Boiled Long-Grain Rice (*see page 214*)

1 Remove the partially frozen beef from the freezer and unwrap the cling film. Using a sharp knife, cut the beef against the grain into 3mm/⅛in slices, or even thinner if possible.

2 Put the beef in a large bowl with the soy sauce, sugar, sesame oil, garlic, ginger and onion and mix well. Cover with cling film and leave to marinate in the fridge for about 1 hour.

3 Meanwhile, heat a frying pan over a medium-high heat, then add the sesame seeds and dry-fry for a few minutes until the seeds begin to pop. Tip onto a plate and leave to one side.

4 Heat the sunflower oil in a ridged griddle pan or heavy-based frying pan over a high heat. When the oil begins to smoke, add the marinated beef and cook for a few seconds before turning the heat down to medium-high. Spread out the meat in the pan, laying it as flat as possible so it cooks evenly. Cook for 10–15 minutes, turning occasionally, until the beef is browned and tender.

5 One minute before the end of cooking, add the spring onions. Sprinkle over the toasted sesame seeds and serve immediately with boiled rice.

sea вream nigirizushi

Nigirizushi is one of the most popular Japanese sushi, and is also called hand-formed sushi, because the rice is pressed and moulded into an oblong shape. I've used short-grain rice because it is readily available and gives a similar texture to sushi rice. It also takes less time to cook, which means these delicious morsels are quick to make. The blushing pink and thinly sliced pieces of sea bream are fresh and great in taste, although you can use other kinds of seafood.

SERVES 4
PREPARATION TIME 15 minutes, plus cooking the rice

200g/7oz boneless, skinless sea bream or sea bass fillet
½ recipe quantity Boiled Short-Grain Rice, cooled (*see page 214*)
1 tsp wasabi

TO SERVE
wasabi
shoyu
Pickled Ginger (*see page 213*)

1 Place the fish fillet horizontally to you on a chopping board. Angle the knife at 45° to the fillet and cut the fillet against the grain into slices of about 3cm/1¼in wide and 3–5mm/⅛–¼in thick.
2 Moisten your hands with water to avoid the rice sticking and scoop up about 1 tablespoon of rice with one hand. Put it in the palm of your other hand and shape the rice into a 5 x 2.5cm/2 x 1in oblong with rounded corners. Take a slice of the prepared sea bream in one hand and smear over a small amount of wasabi. Place the rice on top of the slice of fish, then gently press down on the rice to stick them together. Turn the nigirizushi over and press the top and the sides to make sure the fish is firmly in place. Continue until all the remaining rice and fish is used. Serve with wasabi, shoyu and pickled ginger.

korean-style makizushi

SERVES 4
PREPARATION TIME 45 minutes,
  plus 20 minutes cooling time
COOKING TIME 10 minutes, plus
  cooking the rice

4 tsp sesame seeds
1 recipe quantity Boiled
  Short-Grain Rice
  (*see page 214*)
2 tbsp sesame oil
4 nori sheets (20 x 18cm/
  8 x 7in)

FILLING
2 eggs
1 tsp sunflower oil
200g/7oz baby leaf spinach
½ carrot, cut into matchsticks
½ cucumber, halved
  lengthways, deseeded and
  cut into strips
12 crabsticks
fine sea salt

DIPPING SAUCE
2 tbsp light soy sauce
1 tbsp rice vinegar
generous 1 tbsp lemon juice

1 Heat a frying pan over a medium-high heat, then add the sesame seeds and dry-fry for a few minutes until the seeds begin to pop. Tip half the sesame seeds into a mini food processor and grind to a fine powder. Leave the other half of the sesame seeds to one side.

2 To make the dipping sauce, whisk all the ingredients together with the ground sesame seeds until well combined. Leave to one side.

3 Transfer the cooked rice to a large wooden bowl or a non-metal baking dish. Add the sesame oil and remaining toasted sesame seeds and gently fold through the rice using a spatula. Level the rice, cover with a damp tea towel and leave to cool to room temperature.

4 To make the filling, beat the eggs together with a pinch of salt in a small bowl. Pour the sunflower oil into a large, heavy-based frying pan over a medium-high heat, then use kitchen paper to grease the pan evenly and soak up any excess oil. When the pan is hot, pour in the beaten eggs and turn the heat down to low. Cook the omelette for 3 minutes on each side until cooked through but not coloured. Leave to one side to cool, then cut into strips.

5 Meanwhile, bring a saucepan of salted water to the boil, add the spinach and cook for about 30 seconds. Drain and refresh under running cold water. Squeeze out any excess liquid and pat dry with kitchen paper. Leave to one side.

6 Cover a bamboo sushi mat with cling film and put on a clean surface with a long side closest to you. Leaving a gap of about 2cm/¾in at the edge nearest to you, place a nori sheet, rough side up, on the mat. Moisten one of your hands to help stop the rice sticking to it, then scoop up one-quarter of the rice and spread it evenly over two-thirds of the nori sheet, leaving a small gap at each end. Place 4–6 strips of omelette, a small handful of spinach, 2–3 strips of carrot, 2–3 strips of cucumber and 3 crabsticks horizontally along the middle of the rice.

7 Bring up the bottom edge of the mat, fold it over the filling and then roll the nori up into a cylinder, pressing firmly at the same time to make sure the makizushi is tight and compact. Put a few kernels of cooked rice along the end of the nori sheet and press firmly to seal. Give the mat a final press to create a tight roll. Leave the roll to one side and cover with cling film. Repeat to make 3 more rolls.

8 To finish, lightly moisten the blade of a sharp knife and cut each roll into 5 or 6 rounds. Serve with the dipping sauce.

Tempura Prawn Temaki

When I visit a Japanese restaurant, I always order Tempura and Temaki. Tempura is a dish of seafood or vegetables coated in a light batter, then deep-fried, and Temaki is a cone-like sushi that is pretty to look at and tasty to eat. I've created Tempura Prawn Temaki so that you can enjoy both of these delicious dishes in one!

MAKES 14
PREPARATION TIME 1 hour 35 minutes
COOKING TIME 1 hour, plus cooking the rice

100g/3½oz/heaped ¾ cup plain flour, plus extra for dusting
2 tbsp cornflour
1 tsp baking powder
1 egg yolk
3 tbsp sesame seeds
500ml/17fl oz/2 cups sunflower oil, for deep-frying
14 raw, peeled large king prawns, heads removed, with tails left on and deveined (*see page 216*)
3 tbsp light mayonnaise
2 tbsp lemon juice
1 spring onion, green part only, finely chopped
7 nori sheets (20 x 18cm/ 8 x 7in), halved lengthways
1 recipe quantity Boiled Short-Grain Rice, cooled (*see page 214*)
1 small cucumber, quartered, deseeded and cut into strips
1 small carrot, cut into matchsticks
sea salt

TO SERVE
shoyu
wasabi paste (optional)

1 Mix together the plain flour, cornflour and baking powder in a mixing bowl. In a separate bowl, lightly whisk together the egg yolk and add 160ml/5¼fl oz/⅔ cup ice-cold sparkling water. Pour the egg mixture into the dry ingredients and lightly fold it through using a whisk. Don't overmix the batter – it should stay lumpy. Put the batter bowl into a larger bowl that is half filled with ice cubes to keep the batter cold at all times.

2 Heat a frying pan over a medium-high heat, then add the sesame seeds and dry-fry for a few minutes until the seeds begin to pop. Tip onto a plate and leave to one side.

3 Heat the oil in a deep, heavy-based saucepan to 170°C/325°F or until a small piece of bread turns brown in 20 seconds. Lightly coat each prawn in a little flour, shaking off the excess. Dip the prawn into the batter, then gently slide it into the oil. Fry 2–3 prawns at a time, each one for 2–3 minutes, or until a light golden brown. Remove the prawns, using a slotted spoon, and drain on kitchen paper. Repeat until all the prawns are cooked.

4 Combine the mayonnaise, lemon juice, spring onion and a pinch of salt in a small bowl. To assemble, place a nori sheet on a clean surface with the longest edge closest to you, rough side up. Moisten one of your hands with water, then scoop up about 2 heaped tablespoons of the rice. Spread the rice evenly over the half of the nori sheet closest to you, leaving the bottom corner free of rice also.

5 Spread 1–2 teaspoons of the mayonnaise mixture evenly over the rice and sprinkle over the toasted sesame seeds. Add 1 tempura prawn, 2–3 cucumber strips and 2–3 carrot strips diagonally on top of the rice. Fold the bottom corner of the nori over the ingredients to form a pointed end and then continue to roll to make a cone shape. Stick one or two rice kernels at the corner end and press firmly to seal. Continue until all the ingredients are used. Serve with shoyu, mixed with a little wasabi paste, if you like, for dipping.

soy & mirin tuna on soba noodles

Soba means 'buckwheat' in Japanese and there are two types of soba noodles – the normal dark brown noodle with the natural colour of buckwheat and the green-coloured 'green tea' soba. You can use either, but the green tea version looks very pretty and gives a fresher, lighter taste to the dish.

SERVES 4
PREPARATION TIME 15 minutes, plus 35 minutes cooling and marinating time
COOKING TIME 15 minutes, plus cooking the noodles

400g/14oz skinless tuna
125ml/4fl oz/½ cup shoyu
100ml/3½fl oz/generous ⅓ cup mirin
1 tbsp granulated sugar
1cm/½in piece of root ginger, peeled and finely grated, pulp discarded, reserving the juice
1 tbsp sesame seeds
350g/12oz cooked green tea soba or buckwheat soba noodles (*see page 215*)
1 tsp sunflower oil
1 spring onion, finely chopped, to serve

1 Bring a saucepan of water to the boil, then poach the tuna loin for 25–30 seconds to seal. Remove the tuna from the water, pat dry and transfer to a plate to cool for about 5 minutes.

2 Meanwhile, mix the shoyu, mirin, sugar and ginger juice in a large bowl. Add the seared tuna and thoroughly coat with the marinade. Cover with cling film and leave to marinate in the fridge for 30 minutes.

3 Heat a frying pan over a medium-high heat, then add the sesame seeds and dry-fry for a few minutes until the seeds begin to pop. Tip onto a plate and leave to one side.

4 Remove the tuna from the marinade and strain the marinade into a small saucepan. Simmer the marinade over a medium heat for 2–3 minutes until slightly thickened. Remove from the heat and keep warm.

5 Heat the oil in a large frying pan over a high heat, then add the tuna and sear for 1–2 minute on each side. The outer layer should be cooked and golden brown but the inside should remain raw – don't cook the tuna completely through. Transfer the tuna to a chopping board, angle a sharp knife at 45° to the surface and slice against the grain into 5mm/¼in strips.

6 Meanwhile, while the tuna is searing, bring another saucepan of water to the boil and plunge in the soba noodles for a few seconds to heat through. Drain and divide the noodles into deep soup bowls, then top with the tuna. Drizzle the reduced marinade over the tuna and sprinkle over the toasted sesame seeds and spring onion. Serve hot or cold.

korean spicy seafood noodle soup

SERVES 4–6
PREPARATION TIME 45 minutes
–1 hour, plus making the stock
COOKING TIME 30 minutes, plus
cooking the noodles

1 tbsp sesame seeds
15g/½oz dried wakame
500g/1lb 2oz mussels,
  scrubbed and debearded
1 tbsp sunflower oil
1 onion, sliced
3 garlic cloves, finely chopped
1cm/½in piece of root ginger,
  peeled and finely chopped
4 dried shiitake mushrooms,
  soaked, drained and cut into
  thin strips (*see page 217*)
1 tbsp Korean red pepper
  powder or cayenne pepper
1 recipe quantity Chicken
  Stock (*see page 210*)
¼ Chinese cabbage, core
  removed and cut into
  bite-sized pieces
1 tbsp light soy sauce
1 tbsp Chilli Oil (*see page 211*)
300g/10½oz raw, peeled large
  king prawns, tails left on,
  deveined (*see page 216*)
400g/14oz squid, scored with
  a crisscross pattern and cut
  into bite-sized pieces
  (*see page 216*)
500g/1lb 2oz cooked fresh fine
  egg noodles or 350g/12oz
  dried fine egg noodles (*see
  page 215*)
2 spring onions, finely
  chopped

1 Heat a frying pan over a medium-high heat, then add the sesame
seeds and dry-fry for a few minutes until the seeds begin to pop.
Tip onto a plate and leave to one side.

2 Soak the dried wakame in a small bowl in warm water for about
10 minutes until it rehydrates. Drain, rinse and leave to one side.

3 Tap any mussels that are only partly opened and discard any that
don't shut. Put the mussels in a saucepan over a high heat and steam
for 3–4 minutes, or until the shells open. Discard any that don't
open fully. There is no need to add any additional liquid to the pan,
as the mussels will release their own liquid to steam in. Remove the
mussels from their shells and leave to one side.

4 Heat the sunflower oil in a large saucepan over a medium-high heat.
Add the onion and cook for 2–3 minutes until soft and translucent,
then add the garlic and ginger and cook for 2 minutes, or until
fragrant. Add the shiitake mushrooms and Korean red pepper
powder and cook, stirring continuously, for 1 minute. Remove
from the heat and add the chicken stock.

5 Return the pan to the heat and bring the chicken stock to the boil.
Add the Chinese cabbage and cook for 3–4 minutes until tender.
Add the soy sauce and chilli oil and then add the prawns and squid.
Bring to the boil for a few seconds, then reduce the heat to low,
cover and simmer for 5–6 minutes, or until the prawns turn pink
and are cooked through and the squid is tender. Three minutes
before the end of cooking, add the mussels to heat through.

6 Divide the hot, cooked noodles into deep soup bowls, then
spoon the prawns, squid, cabbage and mussels into the bowls.

7 Bring the chicken stock to a vigorous boil. Add the spring onions
and prepared wakame to the bowls, then ladle in the piping hot
stock. Sprinkle over the toasted sesame seeds and serve
immediately.

Japanese pork dumplings

Growing up in a Chinese family meant that we often made and ate dumplings. I remember lovely times in the kitchen helping my mother to make the wrappers from scratch and prepping the ingredients. As time has passed, dumplings have evolved in my life and I have started using different ingredients such as watercress instead of the usual cabbage to make this dish explode with flavours.

MAKES 28
PREPARATION TIME about 1 hour, plus 1 hour marinating and resting time
COOKING TIME 10–20 minutes

175g/6oz white cabbage, halved and core removed
80g/2¾oz watercress, chopped
5 spring onions, finely chopped
270g/9½oz pork mince
7 garlic cloves, finely chopped
2cm/¾in piece of root ginger, peeled and finely chopped
1 tbsp cornflour
1 tbsp sesame oil
3 tbsp shoyu
1 tbsp sake
1 tsp mirin
1 tsp granulated sugar
1–2 tbsp sunflower oil
freshly ground black pepper

GYOZA WRAPPERS
200g/7oz/scant 1⅔ cups plain flour, plus extra for dusting
sunflower oil, for oiling
sea salt

TO SERVE
shoyu
Chilli Oil (*see page 211* – optional)

1 Bring a large saucepan of water to the boil, add the cabbage leaves and blanch for 1 minute. Remove the leaves with kitchen tongs and plunge immediately into a bowl of ice-cold water to stop the cooking process. Drain, pat dry with kitchen paper, squeezing out as much water as possible, and then finely chop. Transfer to a large bowl and add the watercress and spring onions.

2 Mix together the pork, garlic, ginger, cornflour, sesame oil, shoyu, sake, mirin and sugar in a large bowl until well combined and then season with pepper. Add the cabbage and watercress mix and stir to combine. Cover with cling film and leave to marinate in the fridge for 1 hour.

3 Meanwhile, to make the gyoza wrappers, put the flour and a pinch of salt in a large mixing bowl and make a well in the centre. Slowly pour in 100ml/3½fl oz/generous ⅓ cup cold water and combine with the flour to form a soft dough. Turn the dough out onto a lightly floured surface and knead for 10 minutes until it is smooth and elastic. Shape the dough into a ball, transfer to a lightly oiled bowl, cover with a damp tea towel and leave to rest for 1 hour.

4 Turn the dough out onto a lightly floured surface, roll it into a cylinder and divide into 4–5 equal portions. Take a portion of the dough and roll flat until it is about 2–3mm/¹⁄₁₆–⅛in thick, then, using a 9cm/3½in cookie cutter, cut out neat circles. Dust the surface of the wrappers lightly with flour so they don't stick together, then stack them on a lightly floured plate. Repeat with the remaining dough portions. Keep any dough you are not using covered with a damp tea towel to prevent it from drying out.

5 Have a small bowl of water by the side to use for sealing the dumplings. Place a gyoza wrapper on the forefront of your hand, then put a heaped tablespoon of the pork filling in the centre. Shape the filling into an oblong shape and flatten it slightly. Wet around the edge of the wrapper with water and bring one side of the wrapper over the filling to form a half-moon shape.

6 Press one corner of the wrapper together to seal, then pinch the edge of the top half of the wrapper next to the seal into a pleat, pushing the pleat into the edge of the bottom half of the wrapper to seal. Continue to work around the edge to the other corner. There should be 6–8 pleats and the bottom half of the wrapper should remain flat.

7 When you've finished pleating the pastry, press gently into the back of the pastry to form a crescent shape. Transfer the gyoza to a lightly floured plate and cover with a damp tea towel while you make the remaining dumplings.

8 Heat the sunflower oil in a large frying pan over a medium-high heat, then arrange the gyoza in the pan. Leave a bit of space between each dumpling to avoid the gyoza sticking together. Cook for 3–4 minutes, then pour in enough hot water to half cover the gyoza. Cover and cook over a medium heat until the liquid has evaporated.

9 Remove the lid and cook for a further 4–5 minutes, or until the bottom of the gyoza becomes brown and crisp. Depending on the size of the frying pan, you may need to cook the gyoza in batches. Serve immediately with shoyu and chilli oil, if you like.

PAK CHOI KIMCHI

Kimchi is one of the most well-known side dishes in Korean cuisine, and is served at almost every meal. There are many varieties of kimchi, and how they are made varies from region to region and by season. Varieties from the north tend to be a little less spicy than those from the south, where a lot more Korean red pepper powder is used. While cabbage kimchi is the most common kimchi, other vegetables such as pak choi and cucumber are also often used.

MAKES about 700g/1lb 9oz
PREPARATION TIME 30 minutes, plus 4–5 hours resting time and 2 days pickling

1kg/2lb 4oz pak choi, roughly chopped into 3cm/1¼in pieces
100g/3½oz/½ cup sea salt
3cm/1¼in piece of root ginger, peeled and roughly chopped
6 garlic cloves, roughly chopped
1 onion, roughly chopped
½ red apple, peeled and roughly chopped
30g/1oz Korean red pepper powder or cayenne pepper
2 tbsp granulated sugar
4 spring onions, chopped

1 Put the pak choi in a colander and rinse under running cold water, drain well and transfer to a large bowl or saucepan. Mix the salt together with 500ml/17fl oz/2 cups water until dissolved, then pour the briny liquid over the pak choi. Using both your hands, mix the pak choi and water together, making sure it is well coated with the brine, then leave to stand for 4–5 hours at room temperature.

2 Rinse the pak choi 2–3 times under running cold water to get rid of the brine, then squeeze out the excess liquid and put in a large bowl. Put the ginger, garlic, onion and apple in a food processor or blender and blend until smooth. Transfer the paste to a small bowl and mix in the Korean red pepper powder and sugar. Pour the mixture over the pak choi and tip in the spring onions.

3 Wearing kitchen gloves, thoroughly mix everything together, then transfer the seasoned pak choi to a sterilized preserve jar and seal with a tight-fitting lid. Let the kimchi ferment for 24–48 hours in a cool, dark place before putting in the fridge, where it will keep for up to 1 month. Serve cold.

green tea & sesame seed ice cream

Green tea is a wonderfully versatile ingredient that, apart from making a refreshing hot drink, is an excellent food colouring for natural savoury dishes, cakes and desserts. A bright green ice cream is always a welcome sight on any hot summer day, but with the subtle earthy flavour that comes from the inclusion of toasted ground black sesame, this ice cream is delicious eaten anytime of the year.

SERVES 4
PREPARATION TIME 15 minutes, plus minimum 5–6 hours cooling and freezing time
COOKING TIME 15 minutes

2 tbsp black sesame seeds
500ml/17fl oz/2 cups semi-skimmed milk
100ml/3½fl oz/generous ⅓ cup double cream
2 egg yolks
120g/4¼oz/heaped ½ cup caster sugar
2 tsp green tea powder

1 Heat a frying pan over a medium-high heat, then add the sesame seeds and dry-fry for a few minutes until the seeds begin to pop. Remove from the pan and put in a mini food processor, or use a mortar and pestle, and grind to a coarse powder.

2 Pour the milk and double cream into a saucepan, place over a medium heat and bring just to the boil. Remove from the heat.

3 Meanwhile, using an electric mixer, beat the egg yolks, sugar and green tea powder until light and creamy. With the motor still running, slowly pour in the milk mixture until light and fluffy.

4 Pour the mixture into a clean saucepan over a low heat and cook, stirring continuously, for 10 minutes until it forms a thick custard. Be careful not to overheat or the custard may curdle. Remove from the heat and pour through a fine sieve into a clean bowl. Stir in the ground black sesame seed powder.

5 Leave the custard to cool completely and then pour it into an ice-cream machine. Churn until thick and frozen, according to the manufacturer's instructions, and then transfer to a plastic or metal container, cover and freeze for up to 2 weeks.

CHINA

Chinese cuisine is made up of dishes from the many different regions in China, each varying in taste and appearance. But what is common to all the wonderful dishes that make up Chinese cuisine is the balance of flavours, textures and colours, which are considered to be as important as eating a meal that has a balance of 'Yin' and 'Yang' ingredients. 'Yin' foods, such as Chinese Roast Duck Pancake Rolls (*see pages 42–43*) and the soupy dish, Chinese BBQ Pork Noodle Soup (*see page 45*), are thought to have a cooling effect on the body, whereas 'Yang' foods, such as Beef & Asparagus Stir-Fry (*see page 52*) and Chicken & Sticky Rice in Lotus Leaves (*see page 57*) have warming properties. Rice is one of the staple foods of Chinese cooking. It is always steamed and is served at every meal. Noodles are almost as indispensable as rice, and are normally stir-fried or served in a hot broth.

Key ingredients vary from region to region, but something that is used frequently, everywhere, is fresh ginger, a pungent and spicy root. It lifts the flavour of simple dishes, such as Cantonese Steamed Fish (*see page 54*) and gives depth to other dishes such as Sichuan Mapo Tofu (*see page 48*). Soy sauce is possibly the most important ingredient in Chinese cooking, followed closely by Chinese rice wine. Sesame, Rice Wine & Soy Chicken (*see page 40*) is one very tasty example of a dish that makes good use of both.

sesame, rice wine & soy chicken

This dish originates from the Jiangxi province in southern China, but has become a popular, classic Taiwanese dish. Traditionally, San Bei Ji uses a cup each of sesame oil, rice wine and soy sauce and is simmered in a claypot over a high heat until all the sauce is absorbed by the chicken. I've used a lot less of each to make it less oily and salty.

SERVES 4
PREPARATION TIME 15 minutes
COOKING TIME 25–30 minutes

600g/1lb 5oz boneless, skinless chicken thighs, cut into bite-sized pieces
1 tsp sunflower oil
1cm/½in piece of root ginger, peeled and cut into fine matchsticks
4 garlic cloves, whole and slightly crushed
2 spring onions, cut into 5cm/2in pieces lengthways
2 dried chillies, deseeded and roughly chopped
125ml/4fl oz/½ cup Shaoxing rice wine
3 tbsp light soy sauce
2 tbsp granulated sugar
2 tbsp sesame oil
1 handful of basil leaves
1 handful of coriander leaves

TO SERVE
1 recipe quantity Boiled Long-Grain Rice (*see page 214*)

1 Bring a saucepan of water to the boil and poach the chicken pieces for about 1 minute to seal. Drain and leave to one side.

2 Heat the sunflower oil in a frying pan over a high heat until the oil shimmers and starts to smoke. Add the ginger and stir-fry for 1 minute, then add the garlic and stir-fry for a further 1 minute. Stir in the spring onions, dried chillies and stir-fry for 1 minute. Tip in the chicken, rice wine, soy sauce and sugar, cover the pan and cook for 20–25 minutes until the liquid is evaporated and the chicken is cooked through, stirring occasionally.

3 Meanwhile, heat a claypot or a small heatproof casserole dish over a high heat until very hot. Transfer the chicken pieces from the pan into the claypot, add the sesame oil, basil and coriander and then cover with the lid. Let the chicken sizzle for a few seconds, then serve immediately with boiled rice.

CHINESE ROAST DUCK PANCAKE ROLLS

This is an all-time favourite of mine that never disappoints – tender duck coated with a flavoursome, glistening, soy sauce and golden syrup glaze, served in steamed pancakes. The most important part of the cooking process is resting the duck in an airy place to dehydrate the skin. This drying process results in a delicate, crispy skin when the duck is cooked.

SERVES 4–6
PREPARATION TIME 25 minutes, plus 3–7 hours marinating and resting time
COOKING TIME about 1 hour

1 x 1.8kg/4lb whole duck
1 tbsp sea salt
½ tsp Ground Toasted Sichuan Pepper (*see page 212*)
2 tbsp granulated sugar
1 tbsp Shaoxing rice wine
2 star anise
5cm/2in cinnamon stick
3 spring onions, halved
3cm/1¼in piece of root ginger, peeled and sliced

PANCAKES
250g/9oz/2 cups plain flour, plus extra for dusting
¼ tsp sea salt
1 tbsp sesame oil
sunflower oil, for oiling

GLAZE
1 tbsp golden syrup or honey
1 tbsp granulated sugar
1 tbsp light soy sauce
1 tbsp rice wine vinegar
¼ tsp five-spice powder

1 Rinse the duck thoroughly inside and out under running cold water and pat dry inside and out with kitchen paper. Lightly prick the skin all over with a fork. Rub the salt, Sichuan pepper, sugar and rice wine onto the skin and put the star anise, cinnamon stick, spring onions and ginger in the cavity. Secure the cavity closed with a metal skewer, then transfer the duck to a platter, cover with cling film and leave to marinate in the fridge for about 30 minutes.

2 Bring a large saucepan of water to the boil, then slowly lower in the duck so it is completely submerged. Boil for 5 minutes. Remove the pan from the heat and drain the duck into a colander. Discard the ingredients in the cavity, sit the duck on a wire cooling rack and leave in a well-ventilated area for 5–6 hours, or until all the moisture has evaporated. Alternatively, put in the fridge for 2–3 hours.

3 Meanwhile, to prepare the pancakes, mix the flour and salt together in a large bowl. Gradually pour in 185ml/6fl oz/¾ cup hot water and mix with a wooden spoon until it forms a soft, smooth dough. Add a few extra splashes of cold water if the dough is dry. Turn the dough out onto a lightly floured surface and knead for 10–15 minutes until very smooth, then put in a lightly oiled bowl and cover with a damp tea towel or cling film. Leave to one side for 30 minutes.

4 Pour the sesame oil into a shallow dish. Turn the dough out onto a lightly floured surface, roll it into a cylinder and divide into 8–10 portions of about 30g/1oz each. Take a piece of dough and shape into a ball. Dip the dough in the sesame oil, turning until coated all round, then place the ball on a clean surface and press into a flat disc. Using a rolling pin, roll into an 18cm/7in disc about 2mm/¹⁄₁₆in thick. Place the disc on a lightly floured surface and repeat with the remaining dough portions.

TO SERVE
6 spring onions, cut into fine
   matchsticks
½ cucumber, halved
   lengthways, deseeded and
   cut into strips
hoisin sauce or plum sauce

5 Preheat the oven to 200°C/400°F/Gas 6. To prepare the glaze, mix all the ingredients in a small bowl. Line a baking tray with a sheet of kitchen foil, place an oven rack on top and transfer the duck onto the rack. Using a pastry brush, brush the glaze mixture all over the duck.

6 Turn the duck so the breast is facing down. Position the oven tray on the second lowest shelf in the oven and cook the duck for 15 minutes. After 15 minutes, turn the duck breast-side up. Lower the temperature to 180°C/350°F/Gas 4 and continue to cook the duck for a further 1 hour, or until cooked. After about 45 minutes, brush the glaze mixture all over the duck again. When the tip of a sharp knife is inserted into the thickest part of the meat the juices should run clear. Remove the duck from the oven, pour out any fat or juices from the cavity and leave to one side.

7 Meanwhile, heat a frying pan over a high heat until hot, then reduce the heat to low and cook a pancake for 1–2 minutes on each side until it blisters and light brown spots start to form. Leave to one side, cover with a damp tea towel and cook the remaining pancakes.

8 Steam the pancakes in a bamboo or electric steamer for 5–7 minutes until cooked through just before the duck is ready.

9 Carve the duck meat into slices, removing the skin if it is too fatty, and put on a serving plate with the spring onions, cucumber and hoisin sauce for the pancake rolls to be assembled at the table.

CHINESE BBQ PORK NOODLE SOUP

BBQ pork, known as Char Siu is one of the most popular Guangdong dishes and goes well with rice or noodles. It can also be used as the filling for Chicken & Vegetable Steamed Buns (*see pages 58–59*). For a really tasty dish, marinate the pork well in advance so that the flavours penetrate the meat.

SERVES 4–6
PREPARATION TIME 25 minutes, plus minimum 6 hours marinating time and making the stock
COOKING TIME 50 minutes, plus cooking the noodles

800g/1lb 12oz deboned pork shoulder, skin and excess fat removed
4 tbsp light soy sauce
1 tbsp oyster sauce
2 tbsp granulated sugar
3 tbsp golden syrup or honey
1 tbsp Shaoxing rice wine
3cm/1¼in piece of root ginger, peeled, lightly crushed and sliced
200g/7oz tenderstem broccoli, trimmed
600g/1lb 5oz cooked fresh fine egg noodles or 350g/12oz dried fine egg noodles (*see page 215*)
1 recipe quantity Chicken Stock (*see page 210*)
2 spring onions, sliced
freshly ground black pepper

1 Put the pork in a deep dish or bowl. In a separate bowl, mix together the light soy sauce, oyster sauce, sugar, 2 tablespoons of the golden syrup, rice wine and ginger and season with pepper. Pour the mixture over the pork and then, using your hands, rub the marinade into the pork until it is well coated. Cover with cling film and leave to marinate in the fridge for 6 hours or, for an even better flavour, overnight.

2 Preheat the oven to 180°C/350°F/Gas 4. Remove the pork from the fridge and strain off the marinade, keeping the liquid and discarding the solids. Stir the remaining golden syrup into the marinade. Line an oven tray with kitchen foil, place an oven rack on top and transfer the pork onto the rack. Place the tray on the second lowest shelf in the oven and cook the pork for 25 minutes. Using tongs, turn over the pork and cook for a further 25 minutes, or until cooked. When the tip of a sharp knife is inserted into the thickest part of the meat, the juices should run clear. Five minutes before the end of cooking, generously brush the marinade all over the pork. Remove the pork from the oven and keep warm.

3 Bring a saucepan of water to the boil and blanch the tenderstem broccoli for 2–3 minutes until tender. Meanwhile, divide the warm, cooked noodles into deep serving bowls. Divide the blanched broccoli into the bowls of noodles.

4 Pour the chicken stock into a saucepan and bring to a gentle boil over a medium heat. Meanwhile, transfer the pork to a chopping board and cut against the grain into 5mm/¼in slices. Divide the pork into the soup bowls and sprinkle over the spring onions. Ladle the piping hot stock over the noodles and serve immediately.

dan dan noodles

Egg noodles, topped with pork mince, drizzled with a vinegary sauce and with a hint of spice from chilli oil. A famous dish from Chengdu, vendors used to transport their noodles in baskets hanging from a bamboo pole carried on their shoulders. This means 'dan' in Chinese, giving the dish the name Dan Dan Noodles.

SERVES 4–6
PREPARATION TIME 15 minutes, plus 25 minutes soaking time
COOKING TIME 20–25 minutes, plus cooking the noodles

2 tbsp sunflower oil
1 garlic clove, peeled and finely chopped
1cm/½in piece of root ginger, peeled and finely chopped
20g/¾oz dried mushrooms, such as shiitake, porcini or Chinese mushrooms, soaked, drained and roughly chopped (*see page 217*)
350g/12oz pork mince
2 tsp light soy sauce
1 tbsp sesame oil
1 tbsp Shaoxing rice wine
1 tbsp finely diced carrot
1 tbsp finely sliced green beans
600g/1lb 5oz cooked fresh fine egg noodles or 350g/12oz dried fine egg noodles (*see page 215*)
2 spring onions, finely chopped, to serve

SAUCE
5 tbsp light soy sauce
2 tbsp dark soy sauce
2 tbsp balsamic vinegar

TO SERVE
Chilli Oil (*see page 211 – optional*)

1 To make the sauce, mix together the light and dark soy sauces and vinegar with 4 tablespoons warm water in a small bowl. Leave to one side.

2 Heat 1 tablespoon of the sunflower oil in a frying pan over a medium-high heat. Add the garlic and ginger and fry until they start to turn light golden brown, then add the mushrooms and cook for 1 minute.

3 Add the pork mince, breaking up the lumps. Cook, stirring occasionally, for 5–10 minutes until browned and cooked through, then stir in the soy sauce and sesame oil. Add the rice wine and 3 tablespoons water and simmer for a further 3 minutes. Season with pepper, then leave to one side and keep warm.

4 Meanwhile, heat the remaining 1 tablespoon of oil in a frying pan over a medium heat and stir-fry the carrot and green beans for 1–2 minutes.

5 Divide the cooked noodles into deep soup bowls, then drizzle the sauce mixture over the noodles. Add the pork mixture, carrots and green beans to the bowls, then sprinkle over the spring onions. For a bit of spiciness, add 2–3 teaspoons of the chilli oil, including the chilli flakes, if you like. Serve immediately.

sweet & spicy pork belly

This is a popular dish, regularly cooked in many Chinese households. The method of cooking, however, varies by region. In southern China, the use of dark soy sauce is favoured as it is said it enhances the colour of the dish, whereas in northern China, the colour of the dish is enhanced by the use of sugar, which gives a glossy and caramelized look. A good-quality piece of pork belly is essential to getting the melt-in-your-mouth result that comes from braising the meat in the aromatic sauce.

SERVES 4–6
PREPARATION TIME 15 minutes
COOKING TIME about 1 hour

800g/1lb 12oz pork belly, cut
  into bite-sized pieces
1 tbsp sunflower oil
1 star anise
5cm/2in cinnamon stick
2 dried chillies, deseeded and
  roughly chopped
3 garlic cloves, finely chopped
¼ tsp Sichuan peppercorns
2 tbsp clear honey
2 tbsp light soy sauce
1 tbsp dark soy sauce
1 tbsp Shaoxing rice wine
2 spring onions, cut into
  6cm/2½in lengths
2cm/¾in piece of root ginger,
  peeled and sliced

TO SERVE
1 recipe quantity Boiled
  Long-Grain Rice (*see page
  214*)

1 Bring a saucepan of water to the boil, then lower in the pork belly and poach for 3 minutes to seal. Drain and leave to one side.

2 Heat the oil in a saucepan over a medium-high heat. Add the star anise, cinnamon stick and dried chillies and stir-fry for 2–3 minutes until fragrant. Add the garlic and stir-fry for 1–2 minutes, then add the Sichuan peppercorns and stir-fry for 1 minute, or until fragrant.

3 Add the poached pork belly and mix well, then add the honey, light and dark soy sauces, rice wine, spring onions and ginger. Cook for 5 minutes, stirring occasionally, then add 150ml/5fl oz/scant ⅔ cup water. Bring to the boil and cook for a few seconds.

4 Reduce the heat to low and simmer, covered, for 45 minutes, or until the liquid has reduced and thickened and the pork is tender. Serve hot with boiled rice.

SICHUAN MAPO TOFU

This is a famous Sichuan dish that comes with a story. It is said that during the Qing dynasty, a restaurant on the outskirts of Chengdu was well known for a delicious, very spicy tofu dish, which was made by the restaurateur's wife. She had pockmarks on her face, and as a result was called Mapo – ma means 'pock-mark' and po means 'elderly woman', and her signature dish was called Mapo Dou Fu.

SERVES 4
PREPARATION TIME 10 minutes
COOKING TIME 20 minutes

300g/10½oz soft silken tofu,
   cut into bite-sized cubes
1 tbsp sunflower oil
1 cm/½in piece of root ginger,
   peeled and finely chopped
3 garlic cloves, finely chopped
200g/7oz beef or pork mince
2 tbsp chilli bean paste
1 tbsp light soy sauce
1 tsp granulated sugar
1 tsp Ground Toasted Sichuan
   Pepper (*see page 212*)
1 tsp cornflour
2 spring onions, roughly
   chopped, to serve

TO SERVE
400g/14oz cooked egg
   noodles (*see page 215*)

1 Bring a large saucepan of water to the boil, then remove from the heat. Carefully tip the tofu into the water and leave to one side.

2 Heat the oil in a wok or frying pan over a medium-high heat. Add the ginger and garlic and stir-fry for 1–2 minutes until fragrant but not coloured. Add the beef mince, break up the lumps and cook, stirring occasionally, for 5 minutes, or until starting to brown. Add the chilli bean paste, soy sauce, sugar, ground Sichuan pepper and 200ml/7fl oz/scant 1 cup water, stir to combine and slowly bring to the boil.

3 Carefully drain the tofu and add it to the wok. Gently push the ingredients around the wok until the tofu pieces are coated with the sauce. Do not stir as it may break up the delicate tofu. Let it simmer for 3–5 minutes until heated through.

4 Meanwhile, combine the cornflour with 1 tablespoon water in a small bowl. Slowly pour the cornflour mixture into the wok or pan and gently fold through. Sprinkle over the spring onions and serve immediately with noodles.

sizzling Beef with ginger & spring onions

When I was little, as a Friday evening treat, my parents would often take my sister, brother and me out for dinner. There was a particular restaurant we loved that served lip-smacking frog legs on a cast iron sizzle pan, and it is that mouth-watering dish that is the inspiration behind this sizzling beef dish.

SERVES 4
PREPARATION TIME 10 minutes, plus 40 minutes freezing and marinating time
COOKING TIME 15 minutes

500g/1lb 2oz sirloin, wrapped and semi-frozen for 25 minutes (*see page 217*)
2 tsp cornflour
2 tbsp sunflower oil
2cm/¾in piece of root ginger, peeled and cut into thin matchsticks
2 garlic cloves, finely chopped
2 tbsp Shaoxing rice wine
2 tbsp oyster sauce
3 spring onions, cut lengthways into 6cm/ 2½in pieces
freshly ground black pepper

TO SERVE
1 recipe quantity Boiled Long-Grain Rice (*see page 214)*

1 Remove the partially frozen beef from the freezer and unwrap the cling film. Using a sharp knife, cut the beef against the grain into 5mm/¼in slices. Put the beef in a large bowl with the cornflour and toss together until the beef is well coated. Leave to one side for 15 minutes.

2 Heat 1 tablespoon of the oil in a wok or large frying pan over a high heat until smoking hot. Tip in half the marinated beef and stir-fry for 1 minute, or until sealed all round. Remove the beef from the pan, using a slotted spoon, and drain on kitchen paper. Make sure the wok is still smoking hot, then repeat with the remaining beef.

3 Heat the remaining tablespoon of oil in a clean wok or large frying pan over a medium-high heat. Add the ginger and garlic and stir-fry for 1–2 minutes until fragrant but not coloured. Add the cooked beef slices and toss the ingredients for a few seconds so everything is combined, then add the rice wine, oyster sauce and season with pepper. Cook for 1–2 minutes, tossing occasionally to ensure the ingredients are well combined.

4 Meanwhile, heat a ridged griddle pan, either on the hob or by placing it in a very hot oven for about 5 minutes, until it is smoking hot. If you don't have a ridged griddle pan, use a heatproof dish. Add the spring onions and cook, turning occasionally, for 1–2 minutes until golden brown all over.

5 Pour 60ml/2fl oz/¼ cup water into the wok or pan with the beef. Toss the ingredients so everything is well combined, then bring to a gentle boil for a few seconds and toss again. Transfer the beef stir-fry to the griddle pan and let sizzle for a few seconds. Serve immediately with boiled rice.

Beef & asparagus stir-fry

The wok is an essential piece of equipment in every Chinese kitchen. Its curvy shape means it is hottest at the bottom and enables the heat to rise evenly up the sides. To give your stir-fries some wok hei – which simply means the flavour and aroma imparted by the wok – the wok should be intensely hot before you add the ingredients.

SERVES 4–6
PREPARATION TIME 15 minutes, plus 55 minutes freezing and marinating time
COOKING TIME 10 minutes

500g/1lb 2oz beef fillet, wrapped and semi-frozen for 25 minutes (*see page 217*)
3 tsp cornflour
3 tbsp light soy sauce
1 tbsp dark soy sauce
1 tbsp oyster sauce
1 tbsp sesame oil
2 tbsp Shaoxing rice wine
1 tsp clear honey
3 tbsp sunflower oil
200g/7oz asparagus, cut into bite-sized pieces
¼ tsp freshly ground black pepper
1cm/½in piece of root ginger, peeled and finely chopped
2 garlic cloves, finely chopped
sea salt

TO SERVE
1 recipe quantity Boiled Long-Grain Rice (*see page 214*)

1 Remove the partially frozen beef from the freezer and unwrap the cling film. Using a sharp knife, cut the beef against the grain into 5mm/¼in slices.

2 Put the beef in a large bowl with 2 tablespoons of the cornflour, 1 tablespoon of the light soy sauce, the dark soy sauce, oyster sauce, sesame oil, rice wine and honey and toss until the beef is well coated in the marinade. Cover with cling film and leave to marinate in the fridge for 30 minutes.

3 Heat 1 tablespoon of the sunflower oil in a wok over a high heat until smoking hot. Tip in half the marinated beef and stir-fry for 1 minute, or until sealed all round. Remove the beef from the pan, using a slotted spoon, and drain on kitchen paper. Make sure the wok is still smoking hot, then repeat with the remaining beef.

4 Meanwhile, prepare a large bowl of ice-cold water. Bring a saucepan of water to the boil, add a pinch of salt, tip in the asparagus and cook for 2 minutes, or until al dente. Drain the asparagus and plunge it into the iced water to stop the cooking process.

5 Mix the remaining 2 tablespoons light soy sauce and pepper with 2 tablespoons water in a small bowl. In another bowl, mix together the remaining teaspoon of the cornflour and 1 tablespoon of the sunflower oil, then slowly pour into the soy sauce mixture, stirring continuously.

6 Heat the remaining tablespoon of oil in a clean wok or large frying pan over a medium-high heat. Add the ginger and garlic and stir-fry for 1–2 minutes until fragrant but not coloured. Drain the asparagus and add to the wok and stir-fry for 1 minute. Add the beef and stir-fry for 2 minutes, then add the cornflour mixture. Toss the ingredients so everything is well combined, then bring to a gentle boil for a few seconds. Serve immediately with boiled rice.

Lamb, courgette & orange stir-fry

This dish is light and, with the use of orange and its juice, is fresh-tasting with a touch of citrus sweetness. Traditionally, lamb stir-fries are served with broccoli or asparagus, but here I give it a modern make-over, using courgette instead. The secret to making a delicious stir-fry in minutes is to slice the lamb thinly. It takes less time to cook and the succulent texture is preserved.

SERVES 4–6
PREPARATION TIME 15 minutes, plus 25 minutes freezing time
COOKING TIME 10 minutes

500g/1lb 2oz lamb fillet, wrapped and semi-frozen for 25 minutes (*see page 217*)
2 tsp cornflour
1 tbsp oyster sauce
2 tbsp light soy sauce
1 tbsp dark soy sauce
1 tsp granulated sugar
1 tbsp sunflower oil
1 garlic clove, finely chopped
2–3 spring onions, cut into 5cm/2in lengths
1 red chilli, deseeded and thinly sliced
1 courgette, sliced
½ orange, peeled and cut into bite-sized pieces
150ml/5fl oz/scant ⅔ cup orange juice

TO SERVE
1 recipe quantity Boiled Long-Grain Rice (*see page 214*)

1 Remove the partially frozen lamb fillet from the freezer and unwrap the cling film. Using a sharp knife, cut the lamb against the grain into 5mm/¼in slices. Put the lamb in a bowl with the cornflour, oyster sauce, light and dark soy sauces and sugar and toss until the pieces of lamb are well coated in the sauce. Leave to one side.

2 Heat half of the oil in a wok or large frying pan over a high heat until smoking hot. Tip in the lamb and any liquid and stir-fry for 2 minutes, or until sealed all round. Remove the lamb from the pan, using a slotted spoon, and leave to one side.

3 Heat the remaining oil in the wok or pan over a medium heat, then add the garlic, spring onions and chilli and stir-fry for 1–2 minutes until softened but brown. Add the courgette and stir-fry for about 1 minute, then return the lamb to the wok or pan and stir-fry for a further 2 minutes. Add the orange pieces and juice and bring to a gentle boil for a few seconds. Serve immediately with boiled rice.

cantonese steamed fish

Steaming is one of the most important techniques used in Chinese cooking, and is a very healthy way to cook that retains the flavours of the food, too. A bamboo steamer is ideal, but if you want to steam larger items, such as whole fish, then a wok is handy. In China, the whole fish symbolizes abundance, and steamed whole fish is a must during Chinese New Year, as it symbolizes a wish for abundance in the New Year.

SERVES 4
PREPARATION TIME 20 minutes, plus 45 minutes soaking and marinating time
COOKING TIME 10 minutes

1 x 800g/1lb 12oz whole red snapper, sea bream, sea bass or any other white-flesh fish, scaled and gutted by your fishmonger
1 tomato, sliced
1 tbsp light soy sauce
1 tbsp oyster sauce
1 tbsp sesame oil
2 tbsp Shaoxing rice wine
30g/1oz dried mushrooms, such as shiitake, porcini or Chinese mushrooms, soaked, drained and thinly sliced (*see page 217*)
1cm/½in piece of root ginger, peeled and cut into fine matchsticks
2 spring onions, cut into matchsticks
freshly ground black pepper

TO SERVE
1 recipe quantity Boiled Long-Grain Rice (*see page 214*)

1 Rinse the fish inside and out under running cold water and pat dry with kitchen paper. Using a sharp knife, make three diagonal slits on both sides of the fish. Arrange the tomato on the base of a heatproof platter that will fit inside a wok. Lay the fish on top.

2 Mix together the soy sauce, oyster sauce, sesame oil and rice wine in a small bowl and season with pepper. Pour the sauce over the fish and sprinkle over the mushrooms and ginger. Cover with cling film and leave to marinate in the fridge for about 20 minutes.

3 Place several round cookie cutters or a wire cooling rack with legs at least 2.5cm/1in tall inside a wok. Leaving a minimum gap of 1cm/½in below the steamer, add water to the wok and bring to the boil over a medium-high heat. Set the heatproof plate with the fish on the rack and steam, covered, for 10 minutes, or until the flesh separates from the bone easily and looks opaque when a fork is inserted. Keep an eye on the level of the water, adding more boiling water if necessary. Two minutes before the end of cooking, sprinkle over the spring onions. Serve immediately with boiled rice.

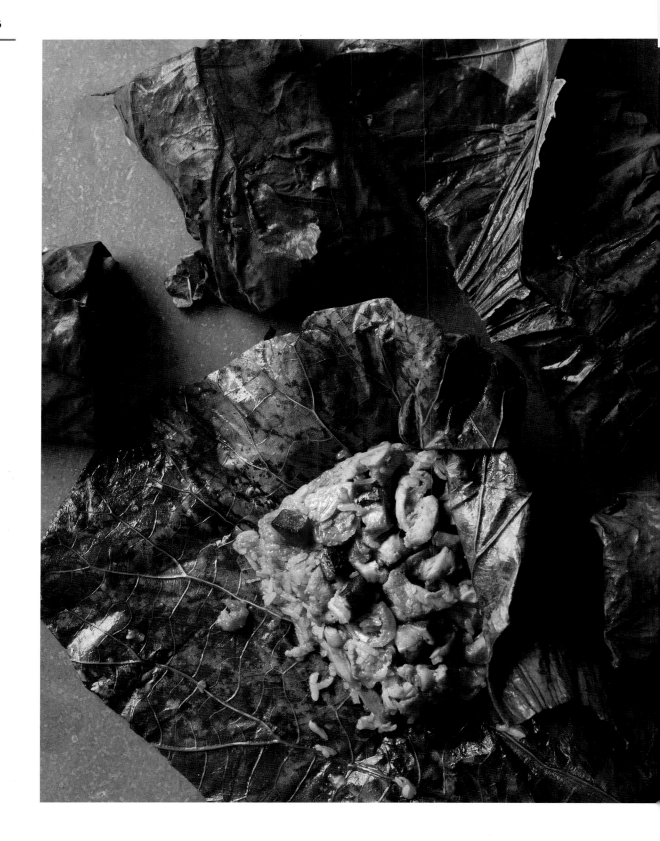

CHICKEN & STICKY RICE IN LOTUS LEAVES

SERVES 4
PREPARATION TIME about
1 hour
COOKING TIME 50–55 minutes

1 tsp granulated sugar
2 tbsp light soy sauce
1 tbsp dark soy sauce
1 tbsp oyster sauce
1 tbsp sesame oil
2cm/¾in piece of root ginger,
    peeled and finely grated, pulp
    discarded, reserving the juice
1 tbsp Shaoxing rice wine
1 tsp cornflour
600g/1lb 5 oz boneless,
    skinless chicken thighs, cut
    into bite-sized pieces
500g/1lb 2oz/2½ cups
    jasmine rice, soaked for
    30 minutes
30g/1oz dried shrimps
1 tbsp sunflower oil
120g/4¼oz air-dried sausage,
    such as Chinese sausage or
    chorizo, diced (optional)
30g/1oz dried mushrooms,
    such as shiitake, porcini or
    Chinese mushrooms, soaked,
    drained and roughly chopped
    (see page 217)
4 dried lotus leaves (optional)
freshly ground black pepper

RICE SEASONING
¼ tsp sea salt
1 tbsp granulated sugar
1 tbsp light soy sauce
2 tbsp dark soy sauce
1 tbsp oyster sauce
2 tbsp sesame oil

1 Mix the sugar, light and dark soy sauces, oyster sauce, sesame oil, ginger juice, rice wine and cornflour in a large bowl until combined, then season with pepper. Add the chicken and toss until each piece of chicken is well coated with the marinade. Cover with cling film and leave to marinate in the fridge for at least 2 hours.

2 Drain the soaking rice and transfer to a bowl. Mix all the rice seasoning ingredients together and season with pepper, then mix through the rice until well combined.

3 Place a sheet of greaseproof paper on the base of a bamboo or electric steamer and spread the rice mixture out on top. Sprinkle over 1 tablespoon water, then steam the rice cake for 30 minutes, or until nicely risen. After 15 minutes, sprinkle over a further 1–2 tablespoons water. Remove the rice cake from the steamer and leave to one side to cool.

4 Meanwhile, put the dried shrimps in a small bowl, cover with water and leave to soak for 15–20 minutes. Drain well and set aside.

5 Heat the sunflower oil in a frying pan over a medium-high heat, then add the air-dried sausage, if using, and stir-fry for 1 minute. Add the mushrooms and shrimps and stir-fry for 2 minutes. Tip in the marinated chicken and cook for 5 minutes, or until the chicken starts to turn opaque, stirring occasionally. Add 3 tablespoons water and cook for a further 3–4 minutes, or until the chicken starts to turn golden brown. Transfer to a bowl and leave to one side.

6 Fill a large saucepan or wok with water and bring to the boil. Slowly submerge the lotus leaves into the water and cook for 1–2 minutes until soft. Refresh under running cold water and pat dry with kitchen paper. Trim off the hard stems and cut the leaves in quarters.

7 To assemble, layer 2 pieces of the lotus leaf together and spoon about 2 heaped tablespoons of rice in the centre. Slightly flatten the rice, then spread 3 heaped tablespoons of the chicken filling evenly over the top. Spoon another heaped tablespoon of rice over the chicken. Fold the bottom side of the leaves over the filling, fold in the two sides and then roll the parcel over to enclose the filling. Continue with the remaining ingredients to make up a total of 8 parcels. The parcels can also be made with greaseproof paper or foil, if preferred.

8 Arrange the parcels in the bamboo or electric steamer and steam for 20–25 minutes until cooked through. Make sure that the heat is maintained throughout the steaming process. Serve immediately.

CHICKEN & VEGETABLE STEAMED BUNS

I use chicken here, but leftover barbecued or roast pork also work. The buns freeze really well, so if you don't need the full quantity, you can freeze them unsteamed. All you then need to do for a delicious dim sum in minutes is to thaw the buns before steaming.

MAKES 25 small buns
PREPARATION TIME 2 hours 45 minutes, plus cooling time
COOKING TIME 20–30 minutes

1 tsp sesame oil
1 tbsp light soy sauce
1 tbsp dark soy sauce
1 tbsp oyster sauce
1 tbsp Shaoxing rice wine
2 tsp granulated sugar
½ tsp cornflour
1 tbsp sesame seeds
350g/12oz boneless, skinless chicken thighs or chicken breasts, trimmed and cut into bite-sized pieces
2 tbsp sunflower oil
2 garlic cloves, finely chopped
1cm/½in piece of root ginger, peeled and finely chopped
1 carrot, cut into matchsticks
200g/7oz Jerusalem artichokes, water chestnuts or jicamas, peeled and cut into matchsticks
2 spring onions, finely chopped
freshly ground black pepper

BUN DOUGH
70g/2½oz caster sugar
1 tsp Shaoxing rice wine
400g/14oz/3¼ cups plain flour, plus extra for dusting
10g/¼oz dried active yeast
2 tsp baking powder

1 Combine the sesame oil, light and dark soy sauces, oyster sauce, rice wine, sugar and cornflour in a large bowl, stirring until the sugar is dissolved. Season with pepper, then add the chicken and toss until each piece of chicken is well coated with the marinade. Cover with cling film and leave to marinate in the fridge for at least 2 hours.

2 To make the bun dough, mix together the sugar, rice wine and 270ml/9½fl oz/generous 1 cup water until the sugar is dissolved. In a large mixing bowl, combine the flour, yeast and baking powder and make a well in the centre. Slowly pour in the sugared liquid and combine with the flour to form a soft dough.

3 Turn the dough out onto a lightly floured surface and knead for 10 minutes until it is smooth and elastic. Shape the dough into a ball, put in a bowl and cover with a damp tea towel. Leave in a warm place for 45 minutes–1 hour until it has doubled in size.

4 Heat 1 tablespoon of the sunflower oil in a frying pan over a medium-high heat. Add the garlic and ginger and cook, stirring occasionally, for 1–2 minutes until fragrant but not coloured. Add the carrot and Jerusalem artichokes and cook for 10 minutes. Add 2 tablespoons water and cook for a further 5–10 minutes until the vegetables have softened. Remove from the heat and leave to cool.

5 Meanwhile, heat a frying pan over a medium heat, then add the sesame seeds and dry-roast until fragrant and starting to brown. Remove and leave to one side. Add the remaining tablespoon of sunflower oil to the pan and heat over a medium-high heat. When hot, add the marinated chicken and cook for 10–15 minutes until golden brown and cooked through. Add the toasted sesame seeds, spring onions and 1 tablespoon water and cook for 1 minute. Remove from the heat and combine with the carrot and Jerusalem artichoke stir-fry. Leave to one side to cool.

6 Turn the dough out onto a lightly floured surface and divide in half. Roll each piece of dough into a cylinder, then divide each cylinder into 25 equal portions. Shape the dough portions into balls, covering them with a damp tea towel as you go so they don't dry out. Leave the balls to rest for 15 minutes. Meanwhile, cut up 25 small squares of greaseproof paper for the buns to rest on when they are cooked.

7 Lightly dust the work surface with flour again, then take a dough ball and flatten it with the palm of your hand. Using a rolling pin, roll the dough into a 10cm/4in disc. Place the disc on the palm of your hand and put 1 heaped tablespoon of the cooled filling in the centre. Gather up the edge of the dough around the filling to create a small bag shape. Twist and pinch together the gathered pleats of dough to seal, then put the bun on a small square of greaseproof paper, pleat-side up, and cover with a damp tea towel. Repeat to make up the remaining buns, then leave the buns to rest for about 30 minutes.

8 Keeping the greaseproof paper beneath the buns, arrange them in a bamboo or electric steamer. Leave a space equal to half the size of a bun between each bun so they don't stick together during cooking. Steam the buns in batches for 5–7 minutes until soft and fluffy to the touch, but not springy. Serve hot.

steamed prawn dumplings

MAKES about 32
PREPARATION TIME 1 hour
30 minutes, plus 1 hour
marinating time
COOKING TIME 15–20 minutes

150g/5½oz raw, peeled large
    king prawns, deveined and
    cut into small cubes (*see
    page 216*)
20g/¾oz bamboo shoots,
    finely chopped
1 tsp cornflour
½ tsp sea salt
½ tsp granulated sugar
½ tsp chicken stock powder
½ tsp sesame oil
freshly ground black pepper

HAR GOW WRAPPERS
200g/7oz/¾ cup wheat starch,
    plus extra for dusting
2 tbsp cornflour
¼ tsp fine sea salt
40ml/1¼fl oz vegetable oil,
    plus extra for oiling

TO SERVE
Chilli Oil (*see page 211*
    – optional)

1 Toss the prawns and bamboo shoots together in a bowl, then add the cornflour and stir in with a wooden spoon. Add the salt, sugar, chicken stock powder and sesame oil and mix until well combined. Season with pepper, cover with cling film and refrigerate for 1 hour.

2 Meanwhile, to make the har gow wrappers, mix together the wheat starch, cornflour and salt in a bowl. Pour in 125ml/4fl oz/½ cup boiling water and stir with a wooden spoon to form a dough. Cover with a damp tea towel and cool for 20 minutes, then add the vegetable oil and knead until the dough is very smooth.

3 Roll the dough into a long sausage shape on a lightly floured surface, then divide it into 32 equal portions. Shape each portion into a ball and flatten slightly between your palms. Place a dough piece on an oiled surface or chopping board and, using a rolling pin, roll into a 9cm/3½in disc. Cut the rolled dough into a neat disc using an 8cm/3¼in cookie cutter, then place the wrapper on a large, lightly floured baking sheet, cover with a damp tea towel and make the remaining wrappers.

4 To assemble the dumplings, place a wrapper on the palm of your hand. Spoon 3–4 heaped teaspoons of the filling in the centre of the wrapper and flatten slightly. Fold the lower edge of the wrapper over the filling to form a half-moon shape, leaving a small gap at the top of the lower half of the wrapper.

5 Pinch the pastry along the curve to seal, then working from one corner of the sealed pastry, use your thumb and index finger to fold over and pinch the pastry together to form a pleat. Continue to work around the edge to the top of the curve, then repeat from the other corner. Each side should have 5–6 pleats, and the underneath of the dumpling should remain flat. Press gently into the base of the pastry to form a crescent shape, then place the dumpling on a lightly oiled plate and cover with a damp tea towel. Repeat for the remaining dumplings.

6 Place a sheet of greaseproof paper on the base of a bamboo or electric steamer and lightly oil. Arrange about 8 dumplings on the paper, leaving a gap between each dumpling so they don't stick together, and steam for 3–4 minutes until cooked through. Repeat until all the dumplings are cooked. Serve immediately with chilli oil, if you like.

sweet peanut & sesame balls

These little gems are generously coated with sesame seeds and have a gorgeous crispy base. The texture of the pastry is slightly chewy and the filling is smooth with crunchy bits from the peanuts. A classic sweet that is still a family favourite.

MAKES 20–22
PREPARATION TIME 50 minutes
COOKING TIME 20–30 minutes

70g/2½oz/scant ⅓ cup caster sugar
320g/11¼oz/heaped 1¾ cups glutinous rice flour, plus extra for dusting
100g/3½oz/scant ⅔ cup skinless raw peanuts
80g/2¾oz/heaped ⅓ cup granulated sugar
500ml/17fl oz/2 cups sunflower oil, for deep-frying
60g/2¼oz/scant ½ cup sesame seeds

1 Add the caster sugar to 250ml/9fl oz/1 cup water and stir until dissolved. Put the rice flour into a large mixing bowl and make a well in the centre. Slowly pour in the sugared water and combine with the flour to form a soft dough. Turn the dough out onto a lightly floured surface, roll it into a cylinder and divide into 20–22 equal portions.

2 Heat a frying pan over a medium-high heat, then add the peanuts and dry-roast until fragrant and starting to brown. Remove from the heat and roughly grind in a food processor or blender – you want a fine powder with some chunky bits. Tip the ground peanuts into a bowl and add the granulated sugar, 2 tablespoons of the oil and 3 tablespoons water. Stir into a rough paste and leave to one side.

3 Fill a small bowl with water and pour the sesame seeds onto a small plate. Take a portion of the dough, shape it into a ball and then press into a 8cm/3¼in disc. Flatten the edges so the centre of the disc is slightly thicker. Spoon 1–2 heaped teaspoons of the peanut paste into the centre of the pastry, gather up the edges and shape into a ball. Repeat for the remaining peanut balls, then dip each ball in the water and coat with the sesame seeds.

4 Heat the oil in a deep, heavy-based saucepan to 170°C/325°F, or until a small piece of bread turns brown in 20 seconds. Gently slide 3–4 sesame balls into the oil and fry for 3–4 minutes until golden brown. Make sure the oil doesn't get too hot so the sesame seeds don't burn and use a slotted spoon to push the balls down into the oil so they cook evenly. Using the slotted spoon, remove the sesame balls from the oil and drain on kitchen paper. Repeat until all the balls are cooked. Serve hot or cold.

PHILIPPINES & INDONESIA

Filipino cuisine is an exotic fusion of Chinese and Spanish cuisines with hints of influences from the Americas and other Asian countries. A popular dish, demonstrating the Chinese influence, is Filipino Prawn & Pork Noodles (*see page 74*). A modern twist here is the use of saffron threads instead of the traditional and common colouring ingredient called achiote seeds. South American influences can be seen in the dish Citrus-Cured Tuna & Tomato Salad (*see page 78*), which is similar to ceviche and uses a number of key ingredients in Filipino cooking, such as chilli, coriander, garlic and ginger. Other storecupboard essentials are fish sauce, vinegar, pepper and tamarind. A dish like Beef, Peanut & Vegetable Stew (*see page 70*) is a good example of Spanish influence, where the techniques of boiling and braising are used.

Indonesia, often referred to as the world's largest archipelago with more than 18,000 islands, also has a rich history and this can be seen in its flavoursome cuisine, which can be hot, sweet, sour and salty, but often has fragrant undertones that come from the use of coconut milk and lemongrass. Both the fresh and dried varieties of the spices coriander, turmeric and chilli play an important role in Indonesian cooking, as do cumin and pepper. The very popular Balinese Fish Satay (*see page 81*) is an example of good use of these aromatic spices, which may be used also as a rub, such as in Balinese Roast Duck in Banana Leaves (*see page 69*), or combined in spice pastes and used in stir-fries such as Indonesian Chicken Fried Rice (*see page 66*).

Indonesian Chicken Fried Rice

SERVES 4
PREPARATION TIME 45 minutes
minutes, plus cooking and chilling
the rice
COOKING TIME 20–25 minutes

1 green bird's eye chilli,
  deseeded and roughly
  chopped
2 red chillies, deseeded and
  roughly chopped
2 shallots, roughly chopped
3 garlic cloves, roughly
  chopped
½ tsp roasted shrimp paste
  (*see page 217*)
1 tsp grated palm sugar or soft
  light brown sugar
60g/2¼oz dried anchovies
2 tbsp sunflower oil
200g/7oz skinless, boneless
  chicken breast, cut into
  bite-sized pieces
80g/2¾oz green beans, finely
  sliced
1 recipe quantity Boiled
  Long-Grain Rice, cooked
  the night before and chilled
  (*see page 214*)
2 tbsp light soy sauce
2 tbsp dark soy sauce
1 tbsp clear honey
1 small handful of coriander
  leaves, finely chopped
sea salt

TO SERVE
1 handful of Indonesian prawn
  crackers (krupuk)
Sambal (*see page 213*)

1 Put the green bird's eye chilli, red chillies, shallots, garlic and shrimp paste in a mortar and pestle or a food processor and blend to a smooth paste. Transfer to a bowl and add a pinch of salt and the sugar. Mix well and leave to one side.

2 Soak the dried anchovies in water for 1–2 minutes, then drain and pat dry with kitchen paper, squeezing out any excess liquid. Heat 1 tablespoon of the oil in a frying pan over a medium-high heat. Add the anchovies and stir-fry for 1–2 minutes until golden brown. Leave to one side.

3 Heat the remaining tablespoon of oil in a wok or large frying pan over a high heat until smoking hot. Add the chilli paste and stir-fry for 3–4 minutes until fragrant. Tip in the chicken pieces and stir-fry for 5 minutes, or until cooked through and starting to turn golden. Add the green beans and cook for about 3 minutes, or until tender.

4 Add the boiled rice, break up any lumps and stir-fry for 5–10 minutes until the chicken is cooked and the rice is hot. Add the light and dark soy sauces and honey and mix in well. Tip in the fried anchovies and coriander and stir until well combined. Serve immediately with the prawn crackers and Sambal on the side.

balinese roast duck in banana leaves

SERVES 4–6
PREPARATION TIME 20 minutes, plus minimum 3 hours marinating time
COOKING TIME 2 hours

1 x 1.8kg/4lb whole duck
enough banana leaves or kitchen foil for wrapping

MARINADE
10 shallots, roughly chopped
6 garlic cloves, roughly chopped
2 lemongrass stalks, outer leaves and stalk ends removed, crushed and roughly chopped
4 kaffir lime leaves, roughly chopped
4cm/1½in piece of root ginger, peeled and roughly chopped
5 red chillies, deseeded and roughly chopped
2 green bird's eye chillies, deseeded and roughly chopped
2 tsp roasted shrimp paste (*see page 217*)
½ tsp black peppercorns
4 macadamia nuts
2cm/¾in piece of fresh turmeric, peeled and roughly chopped or 1 tsp ground turmeric
1 tsp ground coriander
½ tsp ground cumin
1 tsp sea salt
1 tsp clear honey
1 tbsp lime juice

TO SERVE
1 recipe quantity Boiled Long-Grain Rice (*see page 214*)

1 Rinse the duck thoroughly inside and out under running cold water and pat dry inside and out with kitchen paper. Lightly prick the skin all over with a fork.

2 Put all the marinade ingredients in a food processor, except the ground turmeric, if using, coriander, cumin, salt, honey and lime juice and blend to a smooth paste. Transfer to a small bowl and stir in the remaining ingredients. Rub the duck inside and out with the marinade until it is well coated. Layer the banana leaves or kitchen foil on a large plate and wrap up the duck. Secure with cocktail sticks, if necessary. Cover with cling film and leave to marinate in the fridge for 3–4 hours or, for an even better flavour, overnight.

3 Preheat the oven to 200°C/400°F/Gas 6. Put the duck on an oven rack over a baking tray and place on the middle shelf of the oven. Cook for 15 minutes, then reduce the temperature to 180°C/350°F/Gas 4 and continue to cook for 1½–2 hours until cooked. When the tip of a sharp knife is inserted into the thickest part of the meat, the juices should run clear.

4 Unwrap the duck, then using a sharp carving knife, slice the meat into pieces. Serve hot with boiled rice.

beef, peanut & vegetable stew

Traditionally, this Filipino stew is made with oxtail, a variety of vegetables and a peanut spice paste. I have used chuck steak, cut into bite-sized pieces and dry-fried, and ground peanuts. It is a hearty dish made with inexpensive ingredients and is quick to prepare, but it does need some patience while it simmers away, the meat tenderizes and the flavours develop.

SERVES 6
PREPARATION TIME 15 minutes
COOKING TIME about 2 hours 30 minutes

150g/5½oz/scant 1 cup skinless raw peanuts
1.5–1.8kg/3lb 5oz–4lb casserole steak, trimmed of fat and cut into bite-sized pieces
1 tbsp sunflower oil
a large pinch of saffron threads
2 onions, roughly chopped
8 garlic cloves, chopped
1 recipe quantity Kare Kare Spice Paste (*see page 207*)
200g/7oz green beans, trimmed and cut into 6cm/2½in pieces
1 medium aubergine, cut into bite-sized pieces
200g/7oz baby carrots, trimmed
2 tbsp lime juice or 1 recipe quantity Tamarind Water (*see page 217*)
sea salt

TO SERVE
1 recipe quantity Boiled Long-Grain Rice (*see page 214*)

1 Heat a frying pan over a medium-high heat, then add the peanuts and dry-roast until fragrant and starting to brown. Remove from the heat and roughly grind the peanuts in a food processor or blender – you want a fine powder with some chunky bits. Leave to one side.

2 Rinse the beef under running cold water and pat dry with kitchen paper. Heat the oil in a large casserole dish over a medium-high heat, then add half the casserole steak and stir-fry for 4–5 minutes until beginning to brown. Remove the beef from the pan, using a slotted spoon, and drain on kitchen paper. Repeat with the remaining beef, adding more oil as required.

3 Mix together the saffron and 2 tablespoons warm water in a small bowl and leave to one side. Place the casserole dish back over a medium-high heat, then add the onions and garlic and stir-fry for 2 minutes, or until soft and translucent. Add the spice paste and cook gently, stirring occasionally, for 10–15 minutes until fragrant and the oil starts to rise to the surface, then add the beef pieces and combine well. Add the saffron and the soaking liquid and pour in 270ml/9½fl oz/generous 1 cup water. Bring to the boil, cover with a tight-fitting lid, reduce the heat to low and simmer for about 1 hour, skimming off any scum that rises to the surface from time to time.

4 After 1 hour of cooking, tip the ground peanuts, green beans, aubergine, carrots and lime juice into the stew and season with salt. Give it a good stir to coat the vegetables evenly with the mixture and continue to simmer for at least a further 1 hour, or until the beef is almost falling apart and the sauce has thickened. Serve immediately with boiled rice.

makassar beef soup

This soup originates from the island of Sulawesi, Indonesia. It is wonderfully aromatic, with the citrus of the lemongrass and earthiness of spices balancing the richness of the beef perfectly. To make a substantial meal, you can serve it with rice noodles.

SERVES 4–6
PREPARATION TIME 30 minutes, plus 10 minutes cooling time
COOKING TIME about 1 hour

1 x 500g/1lb 2oz beef tenderloin
¼ tsp white peppercorns
1 tbsp granulated sugar
2 lemongrass stalks, outer leaves and stalk ends removed and crushed
1 onion, sliced
2 tsp lime juice
2 tbsp sunflower oil
1 recipe quantity Coto Makassar Spice Paste (*see page 207*)
2 spring onions, finely chopped
1 small handful of coriander leaves, chopped
1 small handful of mint leaves, chopped
2 tbsp Fried Shallot (*see page 212*)

TO SERVE
400g/14oz cooked rice noodles (*see page 215*)

1 Place the beef horizontally on a chopping board, then use a paring knife or a flexible, fine-bladed knife to trim away fat and silver skin. To trim the silver skin, slip the knife between the meat and the silver skin and slide the knife along the length of the beef. Continue this process until all the silver skin is removed.

2 Put the beef, white peppercorns, sugar, lemongrass, onion and 1.75 litres/60fl oz/7 cups water in a large saucepan over a high heat and bring to the boil. Skim any scum from the surface, then reduce the heat to low and simmer gently for 30 minutes.

3 Remove the beef from the stock and leave for 5–10 minutes to cool. Using a sharp knife, cut the tenderloin into strips about 3mm/⅛in thick. Return the meat pieces to the stock, add the lime juice and continue to simmer for 15–20 minutes.

4 Meanwhile, heat the oil in a large frying pan over a medium-high heat. Add the spice paste and cook gently, stirring occasionally, for 10–15 minutes until fragrant and the oil starts to rise to the surface. Pour in the stock and beef and simmer for 10–15 minutes until the beef is tender. Serve immediately sprinkled with rice noodles, spring onions, coriander, mint and fried shallots.

prawn & tamarind soup

When I first tasted this soup it reminded me of the tanginess and spiciness of Prawn Tom Yum Soup (*see page 135*), which got me thinking how a lot of Southeast Asian food shares many similarities. Traditionally, water spinach is used, but I have substituted baby leaf spinach instead. This is a Filipino soup that is rich in colour and flavour.

SERVES 4–6
PREPARATION TIME 15 minutes
COOKING TIME 20 minutes

800g/1lb 12oz raw, unpeeled
　large king prawns
2 shallots, quartered
2 green bird's eye chillies,
　whole
100g/3½oz green beans, cut
　into 5cm/2in pieces
2 tomatoes, skinned and
　quartered (*see page 217*)
1 recipe quantity Tamarind
　Water (*see page 217*)
2 tsp granulated sugar
juice of 1 lime
150g/5½oz baby leaf spinach
sea salt

TO SERVE
400g/14oz cooked rice
　noodles (*see page 215*)

1 Using a pair of kitchen scissors, trim off each prawn the feelers, rostrum, legs and the sharp end of the tail. Make a slit along the back of the prawn with a sharp knife and pull out the black vein with the tip of the knife or your fingers. Rinse the prawns under running cold water and pat dry with kitchen paper.

2 Bring 1.5 litres/52fl oz/6 cups water to the boil in a large saucepan over a medium-high heat. Add the shallots and chillies and cook for 2 minutes, then add the green beans and cook for a further 1–2 minutes. Reduce the heat to low, add the tomatoes and simmer for 2 minutes until the tomatoes begin to soften.

3 Add the prawns and cook, covered, for 4–5 minutes until the prawns turn pink and are cooked through. Add the tamarind water and sugar, then season with salt and add the lime juice, to taste. Bring back to the boil for a few seconds, then add the spinach and cook for 1 minute, or until it starts to wilt. Serve immediately with rice noodles.

FILIPINO prawn & pork noodles

Originally introduced by the Chinese, noodle dishes are a household staple in almost all Filipino homes. In the Chinese culture noodles symbolize longevity, so this dish, which is also a very colourful and festive dish, is a popular choice to serve at birthday celebrations.

SERVES 4–6
PREPARATION TIME 25 minutes
COOKING TIME about
  30 minutes

250g/9oz raw, peeled large
  king prawns, heads removed,
  with tails left on and
  deveined (*see page 216*)
2 tbsp sunflower oil
100g/3½oz firm tofu, cut
  into 2cm/¾in cubes
100g/3½oz pork mince
2 tsp cornflour
a pinch of saffron threads
3 tbsp fish sauce
1 tsp granulated sugar
200g/7oz rice vermicelli,
  soaked according to packet
  instructions
3 hard-boiled eggs, cut into
  wedges
2 tbsp Fried Shallots
  (*see page 212*)
2 spring onions, sliced into
  fine strips lengthways
80g/2¾oz toasted dried
  anchovies (*see page 217*
  – optional)
sea salt and freshly ground
  black pepper

TO SERVE
1 lime, cut into wedges

1 Pour 250ml/9fl oz/1 cup water into a large saucepan and bring to the boil over a medium-high heat. Tip in the prawns and cook until they turn pink and are cooked through. Using a slotted spoon, remove the prawns and keep warm. Reserve the water.

2 Heat 1 tablespoon of the oil in a frying pan over a medium-high heat. Add the tofu and stir-fry for 2–3 minutes until golden brown and crispy all over. Remove from the pan and leave to one side.

3 Reduce the heat to medium and add the remaining 1 tablespoon of oil to the pan. When the oil is hot, add the pork mince, breaking up any lumps. Increase the heat to high and cook for 5–10 minutes, stirring frequently. Meanwhile, mix together the cornflour and 1 tablespoon water in a small bowl.

4 Pour the reserved liquid from the prawns into the pan and bring to the boil over a high heat for a few seconds, then reduce the heat to medium-low. Add the saffron, fish sauce and sugar and season with salt and pepper. Stir in the cornflour mixture and bring back to a gentle boil. Reduce the heat to low and simmer for 5 minutes.

5 Meanwhile, bring plenty of water to the boil in a large saucepan. Drain the soaking rice vermicelli and add to the pan. Cook for 2–3 minutes until softened. Drain the noodles well and put on a serving plate.

6 Bring the simmering sauce to the boil for a few seconds and then remove from the heat. Ladle the sauce over the noodles and divide the fried tofu, prawns and hard-boiled eggs into the bowls. Sprinkle over the fried shallots, spring onions and anchovies, if using. Serve immediately with lime wedges.

gado gado

The main feature of Gado Gado, a popular Indonesian vegetable salad, is the peanut sauce that transforms all the simple ingredients into a harmonious bowl of flavours. And to give it additional crunch, krupuk, Indonesian prawn crackers, are served sprinkled over the top or whole. This salad works well with all sorts of vegetables, so do experiment.

SERVES 4
PREPARATION TIME 1 hour
COOKING TIME about
   30 minutes

150g/5½oz/scant 1 cup
  skinless raw peanuts
3 tbsp sunflower oil
1 recipe quantity Gado Gado
  Spice Paste (*see page 207*)
1 tbsp lime juice or ½ recipe
  quantity Tamarind Water
  (*see page 217*)
2 tbsp granulated sugar
100g/3½oz firm tofu, sliced
150g/5½oz green beans,
  trimmed and cut into 6cm/
  2½in pieces
150g/5½oz/1¼ cups bean
  sprouts or edamame
1 small cucumber, halved
  lengthways, deseeded and
  chunkily sliced
1 small carrot, cut into
  matchsticks
2 hard-boiled eggs, halved
sea salt

TO SERVE
1 handful of Indonesian prawn
  crackers (krupuk)

1 Heat a frying pan over a medium-high heat, then add the peanuts and dry-roast until fragrant and starting to brown. Remove from the heat and roughly grind the peanuts in a food processor or blender – you want a fine powder with some chunky bits. Leave to one side.

2 Heat 1 tablespoon of the oil in a frying pan over a medium-high heat, then add the spice paste and cook, stirring occasionally, for 10–15 minutes until fragrant and the oil starts to rise to the surface. Add the lime juice, sugar, 250ml/9fl oz/1 cup water and season with salt. Tip in the ground peanuts and stir to combine. Bring to the boil, then remove from the heat and keep warm.

3 Meanwhile, heat the remaining 2 tablespoons of oil in a frying pan over a medium-high heat. Add the tofu pieces and shallow-fry for 3–4 minutes until golden brown all round. Remove the tofu with a slotted spoon and drain on kitchen paper. Leave to one side.

4 Bring a large saucepan of water to the boil, then tip in the green beans and cook for 3–4 minutes until tender but still crunchy. Remove from the water with kitchen tongs, refresh under running cold water and leave to one side. Bring the water back to the boil, add the bean sprouts and cook for about 20 seconds. Drain and leave to one side. Serve hot with Indonesian prawn crackers.

CITRUS-CURED TUNA & TOMATO SALAD

Known as Kinilaw in the Philippines, this dish is similar to Ceviche and is usually served as a side dish. The combination of raw fish with all the other aromatic ingredients makes it a very refreshing starter, especially during the summer months. Vinegar is often used to partially cook the fish, but I have substituted it with lime and lemon juice, as I love the freshness they bring to the dish.

SERVES 4
PREPARATION TIME 20 minutes, plus 25 minutes curing time

500g/1lb 2oz skinless, boneless tuna steaks
2 tbsp lime juice
2 tbsp lemon juice
2 tsp granulated sugar
1 garlic clove, grated
5mm/¼in piece of root ginger, peeled and grated
1 green bird's eye chilli, deseeded and finely diced
1 small red onion, finely chopped
2 spring onions, finely sliced
8 cherry tomatoes, quartered
1 small handful of coriander leaves, roughly chopped
sea salt and freshly ground black pepper

1 Place the tuna on a chopping board and cut against the grain into 5mm/¼in slices. Put in a bowl, season with salt and pepper and leave to one side.

2 Mix the lime juice, lemon juice, sugar and a pinch of salt in a small bowl until the sugar is dissolved. Stir in the garlic, ginger, chilli and onion, then pour the sauce over the tuna slices. Toss the tuna until well coated with the dressing, cover with cling film and leave to marinate in the fridge for about 10 minutes.

3 Remove the tuna from the fridge and add the spring onions and cherry tomatoes to the bowl. Return to the fridge to marinate for a further 5 minutes, then remove and leave to stand at room temperature for 10 minutes before serving. Serve with the coriander sprinkled over.

BALINESE FISH SATAY

These satays are great served as party food. They offer something different from the usual beef or chicken satay and are delicious served with Sambal Matah, a Balinese Sambal that is unique because the ingredients are sliced instead of ground to a paste.

MAKES 16
PREPARATION TIME 45 minutes
COOKING TIME about 45 minutes

550g/1lb 4oz skinless, boneless white fish fillets, such as cod, haddock, snapper or whiting
1 recipe quantity Sate Lilit Ikan Spice Paste (*see page 209*)
20g/¾oz freshly grated coconut (*see page 216*) or desiccated coconut
1 tbsp clear honey
16 lemongrass stalks, outer leaves and stalk ends removed
1 tbsp sunflower oil, plus extra for oiling
sea salt

TO SERVE
Sambal Matah (*see page 213*)

1 Cut the fish fillets into bite-sized pieces, then transfer to a food processor. Blend to a smooth paste and transfer to a bowl. Add the spice paste, coconut, honey and a pinch of salt to the bowl and mix until thoroughly combined.

2 Prepare a bowl of slightly salted water. Moisten one hand with the salted water to avoid the fish paste sticking, gather up the fish paste and shape into a ball. Pick up the ball, then slam it down into the bowl a few times until the mixture is glossy and the texture is smooth and springy. Remoisten your hand as necessary.

3 Place 2 heaped tablespoons of the mixture into the centre of a moistened palm. Use the back of the spoon to flatten the mixture into a 5cm/2in circle, then slightly close your hand and place the root end of a lemongrass stalk onto the mixture. Mould the paste around the lemongrass, covering only half the stick. Place the fish satay on a plate and repeat until all the ingredients are used. Brush the fish satay mixture with oil until coated all round.

4 Pour some oil into a ridged griddle pan or heavy-based frying pan over a medium-high heat, then use kitchen paper to grease the pan evenly and soak up any excess oil. Griddle a batch of 5 or 6 satays for 7–10 minutes on each side until golden brown and cooked through. Transfer to a serving plate and keep warm. Oil the pan again, if required, and repeat until all the satays are cooked. Serve hot with the Sambal Matah.

SPICY TOFU

It couldn't be simpler to make this Indonesia-style street food. Originating from West Java, this snack, which is served with a pungent, sweet, sour and spicy sauce, is simply irresistible. For a true Javanese experience, you could replace the firm tofu with tofu puffs, which can be found in Asian supermarkets. They provide a crunchy layer and their spongy centre soaks up all the flavours.

SERVES 4
PREPARATION TIME 20 minutes
COOKING TIME 20 minutes

200ml/7fl oz/scant 1 cup
  sunflower oil
350g/12oz firm tofu, cut into
  bite-sized cubes
1 small cucumber, halved
  lengthways, deseeded and
  sliced into chunks

DRESSING
3 shallots, sliced
2 red bird's eye chillies,
  deseeded and chopped
2 green bird's eye chillies,
  deseeded and chopped
1 garlic clove, finely chopped
3 tbsp grated palm sugar or
  soft light brown sugar
2 tbsp lime juice or 1 recipe
  quantity Tamarind Water
  (*see page 217*)

1 To make the dressing, put the shallots, red and green chillies and garlic in a mortar or food processor and pound with a pestle or blend into a rough paste. Transfer to a bowl. In a separate bowl, mix together the sugar with 2 tablespoons hot water until dissolved. Stir in the lime juice and then the prepared chilli paste. Leave to one side.

2 Heat the oil in a deep, heavy-based saucepan or wok to 180°C/ 350°F or until a small piece of bread turns brown in 15 seconds. Gently slide the tofu into the oil and fry in batches for 10 minutes, or until lightly golden brown. Remove the tofu from the oil, using a slotted spoon, and drain on kitchen paper. Divide the tofu and cucumber onto four plates. Drizzle over the dressing and serve at room temperature.

INDONESIAN SWEET PANCAKES

Known as Martabak Manis, these pancakes can be eaten either savoury or sweet. This classic, sweet version uses coconut milk, which makes them both fragrant and light. For a less traditional version, they could be filled with chocolate chips, fruit or anything else you'd like.

MAKES 5–6
PREPARATION TIME 20 minutes, plus 25–30 minutes resting time
COOKING TIME 45 minutes

75g/2½oz/scant ⅔ cup self-raising flour
55g/2oz/scant ⅓ cup rice flour
1 tsp baking powder
½ tsp instant yeast powder
100g/3½oz/scant ½ cup caster sugar
1 egg
125ml/4fl oz/½ cup coconut milk

FILLING
75g/2½oz/½ cup raw cashew nuts
40g/1½oz butter or margarine, softened and cut into cubes, plus extra for greasing
55g/2oz/¼ cup granulated sugar
75g/2½oz/scant 1 cup desiccated coconut

1 Combine the self-raising flour, rice flour, baking powder, instant yeast powder and caster sugar in a mixing bowl. Crack in the egg and stir until combined. In a separate jug or bowl, mix together the coconut milk and 100ml/3½fl oz/⅓ cup + 2 tbsp water, then slowly pour into the dry ingredients and mix to a smooth batter. Leave at room temperature for 25–30 minutes.

2 Meanwhile, heat a frying pan over a medium-high heat, then add the cashew nuts and dry-roast until fragrant and starting to brown. Remove from the heat and roughly grind in a food processor or blender – you want a fine powder with some chunky bits.

3 Heat a 18cm/7in heavy-based frying pan over a medium heat and lightly grease with butter. Spoon a ladleful of the batter into the centre of the pan, then swirl the pan to cover the base with the batter. Cook the pancake for 3–4 minutes, or until little bubbles start to form on the surface.

4 Put a knob of the butter on the pancake and sprinkle over 2 teaspoons of the granulated sugar, 1 tablespoon of the ground cashews and 1 tablespoon of the desiccated coconut. Use a spatula to check the pancake is golden brown underneath, then transfer to a plate and fold it in half. Leave to one side and keep warm while you make the remaining 4 or 5 pancakes. Serve hot.

steameD rIce cakes

Steamed Rice Cakes, known as Puto, are a traditional Filipino dessert. The most popular natural colouring for these is extract of Pandan leaves, which is usually used for its bright green colour and its sweet fragrance. However, I've used green tea powder because it is much easier to prepare. Usually eaten as an afternoon snack with a cup of tea or coffee, it is also often served during breakfast.

MAKES 12
PREPARATION TIME 20 minutes, plus 30 minutes resting time
COOKING TIME 15 minutes

300g/10½oz/scant 1⅔ cups rice flour
150g/5½oz/scant 1¼ cups self-raising flour
1 tbsp baking powder
1 tsp instant yeast powder
190g/6¾oz/heaped ¾ cup caster sugar
a pinch of sea salt
400ml/14fl oz/1½ cups + 2 tbsp coconut milk
1½ tsp green tea powder, for colouring
2 tbsp freshly grated coconut (*see page 216*) or desiccated coconut, to serve
grated palm sugar or soft light brown sugar, to serve (optional)

1 Combine the rice flour, self-raising flour, baking powder, instant yeast powder, sugar and salt in a mixing bowl. Add the coconut milk and 3 tablespoons water and stir until the sugar is dissolved. Pour half of the mixture into a separate bowl, add the green tea powder and mix well. Leave both the green and white mixture to stand at room temperature for 30 minutes.

2 Divide the white mixture into six individual muffin moulds or 100ml/3½fl oz/generous ⅓ cup ramekins. Repeat with the green mixture to give a total of 12 rice cakes.

3 Arrange the moulds in a bamboo or electric steamer and steam for 15 minutes, or until the cakes are nicely risen. Depending on the size of the steamer, you may need to cook the rice cakes in batches. Serve hot or cold with the coconut scattered over and a sprinkling of sugar, if you like.

MALAYSIA & SINGAPORE

Malaysian food is like an array of delicious foods that reflects the country's different ethnic backgrounds – Malay, Chinese, Indian, Nyonya, Eurasian and the indigenous people of Borneo. Beef Rendang (*see page 100*) is a delicious example of the harmonious mix of Indian and Malaysian cuisines, and the spicy, sweet, sour and salty tastes in Penang Assam Laksa (*see page 102*) show the natural fusion of Malaysian, Nyonya and Chinese ingredients and cooking techniques. The spice trade in the 15th century brought many different exotic spices to Malaysia, including cardamom, cinnamon, clove and star anise, and these are still popular spices to cook with and are all used to make Malaysian Chicken Red Curry (*see page 92*), for example.

Singapore was an important port for the spice trade during the British occupation, and this, along with the different ethnic groups, has also resulted in a rich and strong food culture. Along with the different spices used, such as cinnamon, coriander, cumin, fennel and five-spice powder, other flavourings often used are chilli, ginger, garlic, shallots, soy sauce and shrimp paste, as used in the mouth-watering Singaporean Chilli Crab (*see page 109*). Another dish that provides a delicious all-round example of the flavours and style of Singaporean food, and the strong influence of Chinese cuisine, is Pork & Mushroom Noodles (*see page 96*).

claypot chicken rice

If you can, cook this dish the traditional way in a claypot. You will get to enjoy a particularly crunchy layer of rice, which will form at the base and is an important characteristic of the dish. The combination of fluffy and crunchy rice, chicken generously coated in a tasty sauce and the earthy flavour of Chinese mushrooms makes this a mouth-watering and satisfying dish.

SERVES 4
PREPARATION TIME 20 minutes, plus 40 minutes marinating and soaking time
COOKING TIME 30–35 minutes

700g/1lb 9oz chicken drumsticks or 500g/1lb 2oz skinless, boneless chicken thighs, cut into bite-sized pieces
1 tbsp sesame oil
1 tbsp oyster sauce
2 tbsp light soy sauce
2 tbsp dark soy sauce
1 tbsp Shaoxing rice wine
1 tbsp clear honey
3cm/1¼in piece of root ginger, peeled and finely grated, pulp discarded, reserving the juice
350g/12oz/1¾ cups Long-Grain Rice, soaked and rested (*see page 214*)
2 tbsp sunflower oil
4 dried Chinese mushrooms, soaked, drained and sliced into thin strips (*see page 217*)
2 spring onions, finely sliced
2 red bird's eye chillies, finely sliced, to serve (optional)
freshly ground black pepper

1 If using chicken drumsticks, rinse the drumsticks under running cold water and pat dry with kitchen paper. Remove the skin and then, using a large chef's knife, cut each drumstick into 2 pieces through the bone. Put the drumstick pieces or thighs, if using, into a large bowl and add the sesame oil, oyster sauce, light and dark soy sauces, rice wine, honey and ginger juice and season with pepper. Toss until each piece of chicken is well coated with the marinade, then cover with cling film and leave to marinate at room temperature for 30 minutes.

2 Put the rice in a claypot or deep, heavy-based saucepan. Place the pot over a high heat, pour in 455ml/16fl oz/scant 2 cups water and bring to the boil. Stir well, then reduce the heat to low, cover and simmer for 10 minutes.

3 Meanwhile, heat the sunflower oil in a frying pan over a medium-high heat. Add the mushrooms and stir-fry for 1 minute, then remove with a slotted spoon and leave to one side. Add the marinated chicken to the pan, reserving the marinade, and cook, stirring occasionally, for 10–12 minutes until almost cooked and browned. Leave to one side.

4 After the rice has simmered for 10 minutes and the liquid is almost absorbed, spread the chicken pieces and mushrooms on top of the rice. Cover and continue to cook over a very low heat for another 15 minutes, or until the chicken is cooked through. Add the reserved marinade and cook for 4–5 minutes, then add in the spring onions and cook for a further 1 minute. Serve immediately with the chilli slices sprinkled over, if you like.

Hainanese chicken rice

SERVES 4–6
PREPARATION TIME 1 hour
15 minutes
COOKING TIME 45 minutes

1 x 1.5kg/3lb 5oz whole
  chicken
1 tbsp sunflower oil
2cm/¾in piece of root ginger,
  peeled and finely chopped
1 garlic clove, finely chopped
2 shallots, thinly sliced
½ tsp sea salt
350g/12oz/1¾ cups long-
  grain rice, soaked and rested
3 lemongrass stalks, outer
  leaves and stalk ends
  removed and crushed
1 spring onion, finely chopped,
  to serve
1 small cucumber, halved
  lengthways, deseeded and
  sliced, to serve

CHILLI DIPPING SAUCE
5 large red chillies, roughly
  chopped
2 red bird's eye chillies,
  deseeded and roughly
  chopped
3 garlic cloves, roughly
  chopped
1cm/½in piece of root ginger,
  peeled and grated
1¼ tbsp granulated sugar
2 tbsp light soy sauce
½ tsp sea salt
2 tbsp lime juice

BASIL DIPPING SAUCE
55g/2oz Thai basil leaves
1 green bird's eye chilli,
  deseeded and roughly
  chopped
4 garlic cloves, roughly
  chopped
1 tsp sunflower oil
sea salt

1 To make the chilli dipping sauce, put the chillies, garlic and ginger into a food processor and blend to a smooth paste. Transfer to a small bowl, add the sugar and stir until dissolved. Stir in the soy sauce, salt and lime juice and leave to one side.

2 To make the basil dipping sauce, put the Thai basil leaves, chilli and garlic into a food processor and blend to a smooth paste. Transfer to a small bowl, add a pinch of salt and stir in the oil. Leave to one side.

3 Rinse the chicken thoroughly inside and out under running cold water and pat dry inside and out with kitchen paper.

4 Half fill a large, heavy-based saucepan with water and bring to the boil over a high heat. Add the chicken, breast-side down, and boil for about 20 seconds. Reduce the heat to low, cover and simmer for 15 minutes. Skim any scum or fat from the surface, turn over the chicken, cover again and continue to cook for 10–15 minutes until the chicken is cooked. When the tip of a sharp knife is inserted into the thickest part of the meat, the juices should run clear.

5 Remove the chicken from the stock and leave until it is cool enough to handle. Leave the chicken stock in the saucepan but turn off the heat. Using a pair of poultry scissors or a large sharp knife, cut the chicken into 12–18 pieces, as preferred.

6 Meanwhile, heat the oil in a saucepan over a medium-high heat. Add the ginger, garlic and shallots and cook, stirring occasionally, for 5–7 minutes until fragrant but not coloured. Add the salt and rice and stir-fry for 1–2 minutes. Pour in 455ml/16fl oz/scant 2 cups of the chicken stock and add the lemongrass. Bring to the boil, then stir with a wooden spoon to prevent the rice sticking to the base of the pan. Reduce the heat to low, cover and simmer gently for 20 minutes.

7 Remove the pan from the heat, leaving the lid tightly closed, and leave to steam for 10–15 minutes until cooked. Fluff the rice with a fork and discard the lemongrass. Meanwhile, bring the remaining chicken stock to the boil.

8 Divide the rice into individual bowls and top with the chicken pieces. Ladle in the chicken stock and sprinkle over the spring onions. Serve with the cucumber, chilli dipping sauce and basil dipping sauce on the side.

CHICKEN & Prawn Laksa

SERVES 4–6
PREPARATION TIME 45 minutes
COOKING TIME 1 hour
30 minutes, plus cooking the
noodles

600g/1lb 5oz chicken
  drumsticks, skin and excess
  fat removed
500g/1lb 2oz raw, peeled large
  king prawns, deveined (*see
  page 216*)
2 tbsp sunflower oil
2 sprigs curry leaves, roughly
  chopped (optional)
1 recipe quantity Laksa Spice
  Paste (*see page 206*)
500ml/17fl oz/2 cups coconut
  milk
300g/10½oz cooked fresh egg
  noodles or 250g/9oz dried
  fine egg noodles (*see page
  215*)
200g/7oz cooked dried rice
  vermicelli (*see page 215*)
100g/3½oz Chinese long
  beans or green beans,
  trimmed and cut into
  5cm/2in lengths
200g/7oz/2 cups bean sprouts
200g/7oz firm tofu, fried
2 hard-boiled eggs, quartered
sea salt

TO SERVE
Chilli Paste (*see page 212*
  – optional)

1 Pour 1.5 litres/52fl oz/6 cups water into a large, heavy-based saucepan and bring to the boil over a medium-high heat. Add the chicken drumsticks and boil for about 10 minutes, then reduce the heat to low, cover and simmer for about 10 minutes. Skim off any scum or fat from the surface and continue to simmer for 10–15 minutes until cooked. When the tip of a sharp knife is inserted into the thickest part of the meat, the juices should run clear. Remove the drumsticks, using a pair of tongs, and leave to one side until cool enough to handle. Leave the chicken stock simmering in the saucepan.

2 Cut the meat off the drumsticks, then shred or slice the meat. Cover with cling film and leave to one side. Return the bones to the stock, reduce the heat to low and continue to simmer for 30 minutes.

3 Meanwhile, transfer 300ml/10½fl oz/scant 1¼ cups of the chicken stock into a separate saucepan and bring to the boil over a medium-high heat. Add the prawns and cook until they turn pink and are cooked through. Using a slotted spoon, remove the prawns from the stock, drain on kitchen paper and leave to one side. Return the prawn-flavoured stock to the main pan of simmering chicken stock.

4 Heat the oil in a frying pan over a medium-high heat. Add the curry leaves, if using, and fry for 1–2 minutes until fragrant. Add the spice paste and cook gently, stirring occasionally, for 10–15 minutes until fragrant and the oil starts to rise to the surface. Remove the curry leaves from the pan, then pour the paste into the stock. Add the coconut milk to the stock and season with salt.

5 Divide the warm, cooked egg noodles and rice vermicelli into deep soup bowls. Bring a saucepan of water to the boil and blanch the Chinese long beans for 1 minute then, using a pair of tongs, remove the beans and divide into the bowls of noodles. Return the water to the boil and blanch the bean sprouts for about 20 seconds. Drain and divide into the bowls with the noodles and beans.

6 Divide the shredded chicken, prawns, tofu and hard-boiled eggs into the bowls on top of the bean sprouts. Bring the stock to a vigorous boil, then ladle into the bowls. Serve immediately with chilli paste on the side, if you like.

malaysasian chicken red curry

When I was learning to cook, my mum shared with me a tip that she said would ensure my aromatic curries will always be a success: empat sekawan or the 'four buddies' – star anise, green cardamom, clove and cinnamon. Used here with the spice paste, I guarantee you that this will be one of the most aromatic and delicious red curries you will ever eat.

SERVES 4–6
PREPARATION TIME 45 minutes, plus 2 hours 30 minutes marinating and resting time
COOKING TIME 2 hours 15 minutes

1kg/2lb 4oz chicken drumsticks, skin and excess fat removed
1 tbsp turmeric
500ml/17fl oz/2 cups sunflower oil, for deep-frying
2 red onions, sliced into rings
4 green cardamoms
2 star anise
2 cloves
6cm/2½in cinnamon stick
1 recipe quantity Ayam Masak Merah Spice Paste (*see page 206*)
4 tomatoes, skinned and quartered (*see page 217*)
2 tbsp lime juice or 1 recipe quantity Tamarind Water (*see page 217*)
2 tbsp tomato purée
3 tbsp tomato ketchup
1 tsp dark soy sauce
3 tbsp granulated sugar
sea salt

TO SERVE
1 recipe quantity Boiled Long-Grain Rice (*see page 214* – optional)

1 Season the chicken drumsticks with salt and lightly coat with the turmeric. Cover with cling film and leave to marinate in the fridge for about 2 hours.

2 Remove the chicken from the fridge and leave to stand at room temperature for about 30 minutes before deep-frying. Heat 455ml/16fl oz/scant 2 cups of the oil in a wok or deep, heavy-based saucepan to 180°C/350°F or until a small piece of bread turns brown in 15 seconds. Fry the chicken drumsticks in batches for about 15 minutes until they turn golden brown. Don't overcrowd the wok or pan, as this will lower the temperature of the oil. Remove the drumsticks from the oil with kitchen tongs and drain on kitchen paper or a wire cooling rack and leave to one side.

3 Heat the remaining oil in a saucepan over a medium heat. Add the onions, cardamoms, star anise, cloves and cinnamon stick and cook until the onion is soft and translucent. Add the spice paste and cook gently, stirring occasionally, for 10–15 minutes until fragrant and the oil starts to rise to the surface. Stir in the tomatoes and cook for about a further 5 minutes.

4 Add the lime juice and 100ml/3½fl oz/generous ⅓ cup water and bring to the boil. Reduce the heat to low and simmer for 15 minutes. Stir in the tomato purée, tomato ketchup, soy sauce and sugar and season with salt.

5 Add the fried chicken pieces to the pan and push around the pan with a wooden spoon until they are well coated with the sauce. Increase the heat to high and bring to the boil, then reduce the heat to medium-low, cover and cook, stirring occasionally, for 40 minutes, or until the chicken is cooked through and the sauce has thickened. Serve immediately with boiled rice, if you like.

nyonya Fried Chicken

This is a fantastic, easy-to-make Baba-Nyonya influenced dish. If you can, marinate the chicken overnight so you get to enjoy the full impact of flavours and especially tender chicken. The Worcestershire sauce used in the dipping sauce is an example of the colonial influences in Malaysian cuisine.

SERVES 4–6
PREPARATION TIME 30 minutes, plus minimum 4 hours 30 minutes marinating and resting time
COOKING TIME 20 minutes

5 shallots, roughly chopped
1 tbsp ground coriander
1 tsp ground cumin
1 tsp turmeric
1 egg yolk
1 tbsp cornflour
2 tsp honey
1¼ tsp sea salt
2cm/¾in piece of root ginger, peeled and finely grated, pulp discarded, reserving the juice
1kg/2lb 4oz chicken drumsticks, excess fat removed
500ml/17fl oz/2 cups sunflower oil, for deep-frying
freshly ground black pepper

DIPPING SAUCE
1 tbsp Worcestershire sauce
1 tbsp granulated sugar
1 tbsp light soy sauce
1 red bird's eye chilli, deseeded and finely sliced
juice of 1 lime

TO SERVE
1 recipe quantity Boiled Long-Grain Rice (*see page 214*)

1 Put the shallots in a mortar and pestle or a food processor and blend to a smooth paste. Transfer to a large bowl and add the coriander, cumin, turmeric, egg yolk, cornflour, honey, sea salt and ginger juice and season with pepper. Stir to mix well. Tip in the chicken drumsticks and toss until each piece of chicken is well coated in the marinade. Cover with cling film and leave to marinate in the fridge for at least 4 hours or, for an even better flavour, overnight.

2 Remove the chicken from the fridge and leave to stand at room temperature for about 30 minutes before deep-frying. Meanwhile, in a small bowl, mix together the dipping sauce ingredients and leave to one side.

3 Heat the oil in a deep, heavy-based saucepan to 180°C/350°F or until a small piece of bread turns brown in 15 seconds. Gently slide half the drumsticks into the oil and fry for 10 minutes, or until the the meat is cooked through and the skin crispy. Remove the drumsticks with kitchen tongs and drain on kitchen paper or a wire cooking rack, keeping warm. Make sure the oil is still hot, then repeat with the remaining drumsticks. Alternatively, bake the drumsticks in a preheated oven, 200°C/400°F/Gas 6, for about 20 minutes until cooked through. Serve hot with boiled rice and the dipping sauce on the side.

pork & mushroom noodles

There are many ways of serving noodles, but the two most common are either in a soup or tossed in a sauce (with a soup served on the side). The latter is referred to as 'dry' noodles and Bak Chor Mee is a great example. This dish is of southern China origin, and is popular in both Malaysia and Singapore. Over time it has evolved, and one of the changes is serving it with Sambal – a chilli-based sauce.

SERVES 4
PREPARATION TIME 20 minutes, plus 25 minutes soaking time
COOKING TIME 15 minutes, plus cooking the noodles

1 tbsp sunflower oil
2 garlic cloves, finely chopped
30g/1¼oz dried mushrooms, such as shiitake, porcini or Chinese mushrooms, soaked, drained and roughly chopped, and liquid reserved (*see page 217*)
350g/12oz pork mince
150g/5½oz/1¼ cups bean sprouts or mixed sprouts
300g/10½oz cooked dried egg noodles (*see page 215*)
freshly ground black pepper
2 spring onions, sliced into thin strips lengthways, to serve

SAUCE
3 tsp clear honey
5 tbsp light soy sauce
2 tbsp dark soy sauce
1 tbsp sesame oil
4½ tsp balsamic vinegar

TO SERVE
Sambal (*see page 213* – optional)

1 To make the sauce, combine all the ingredients with 2 tablespoons warm water in a small bowl. Season with pepper and set aside.

2 Heat the sunflower oil in a frying pan over a medium-high heat. Add the garlic and stir-fry for 1–2 minutes, or until fragrant. Add the mushrooms and stir-fry for 1 minute. Tip in the pork mince and break up any lumps. Add 5 tablespoons of the mushroom liquid, season with pepper and cook, stirring occasionally, for 5–7 minutes until the pork is cooked through. Remove from the heat and keep warm.

3 Bring a saucepan of water to the boil and blanch the bean sprouts for about 20 seconds. Divide the warm, cooked noodles on to serving dishes, then top with the blanched bean sprouts. Spoon the sauce over the noodles and bean sprouts, then spoon over the pork and mushroom mixture. Sprinkle over the spring onions, add 1 heaped teaspoon of Sambal to each bowl, if using, and serve immediately.

Braised pork ribs

This is a dish that I will always remember eating as a child. My mum still makes it often, and always with more chilli than is normal to give the sauce a bigger kick. Barbecuing is a popular way to cook spare ribs, but another way, which I think is much better and use here, is braising – slowly cooking the ribs in a broth until the meat is so tender it almost falls off the bones.

SERVES 4
PREPARATION TIME 15 minutes
COOKING TIME 2 hours
  15 minutes

800g/1lb 12oz pork ribs, cut
  lengthways into 4cm/1½in
  pieces
1 tbsp sunflower oil
4 garlic cloves, finely chopped
2 red chillies, deseeded and
  sliced
1cm/½in piece of root ginger,
  peeled and finely chopped
3 tbsp Chinese fermented
  soybean paste
1 tbsp Shaoxing rice wine
1 tbsp dark soy sauce
1 tbsp lime juice or ½ recipe
  quantity Tamarind Water
  (*see page 217*)
1 tsp honey
1 spring onion, thinly sliced on
  the diagonal, to serve

TO SERVE
400g/14oz cooked rice
  noodles (*see page 215*)

1 Bring a large saucepan of water to the boil, then carefully tip in the pork ribs and poach for 1–2 minutes until sealed. Drain the ribs into a colander, rinse the ribs under running cold water to stop the cooking process and leave to one side.

2 Heat the oil in a large saucepan over a medium-high heat. Add the garlic, chillies and ginger and stir-fry for 2–3 minutes until fragrant but not coloured. Add the pork ribs and push around the pan until well coated with the spices. Add the soybean paste, rice wine, soy sauce, lime juice and honey and stir thoroughly.

3 Add 250ml/9fl oz/1 cup water to the pan and bring to the boil. Reduce the heat to low and simmer, covered, for 2 hours until the meat is very tender and almost falls apart. Sprinkle with the spring onion and serve immediately.

beef rendang

Beef Rendang is one of those classic curries where the extra effort of making the spice paste from scratch is absolutely worthwhile. Although a Rendang can be made with lamb or chicken, the rich and thick sauce goes especially well with beef.

SERVES 4–6
PREPARATION TIME 30 minutes
COOKING TIME about 2 hours 45 minutes

55g/2oz freshly grated coconut (*see page 216*) or 40g/1½oz/scant ½ cup desiccated coconut
3 tbsp sunflower oil
1 recipe quantity Rendang Spice Paste (*see page 209*)
1kg/2lb 4oz casserole steak, trimmed of fat and cut into bite-sized pieces
2 tbsp lime juice or 1 recipe quantity Tamarind Water (*see page 217*)
2 lemongrass stalks, outer leaves and stalk ends removed and crushed
5 kaffir lime leaves, bruised
2 tbsp grated palm sugar or soft light brown sugar
400ml/14fl oz/generous 1½ cups coconut milk
sea salt

TO SERVE
1 recipe quantity Boiled Long-Grain Rice (*see page 214*)

1 Heat a frying pan over a medium heat and dry-fry the coconut for 3–5 minutes until light golden brown, stirring occasionally. Leave to one side.

2 Heat the oil in a large casserole pot or a wok over a medium-high heat. Add the spice paste and cook gently, stirring occasionally, for 10–15 minutes until fragrant and the oil starts to rise to the surface. Tip the beef into the pan, stir until well coated, then cook for 5–10 minutes until sealed and beginning to brown.

3 Add the lime juice, lemongrass, kaffir lime leaves, sugar and coconut milk and season with salt. Bring to the boil, then reduce the heat to low and simmer, uncovered, for 2–2½ hours until tender and the meat is falling apart. During the last 45 minutes of cooking stir more frequently. When the liquid starts to thicken, add in the toasted coconut and mix well. Serve immediately with boiled rice.

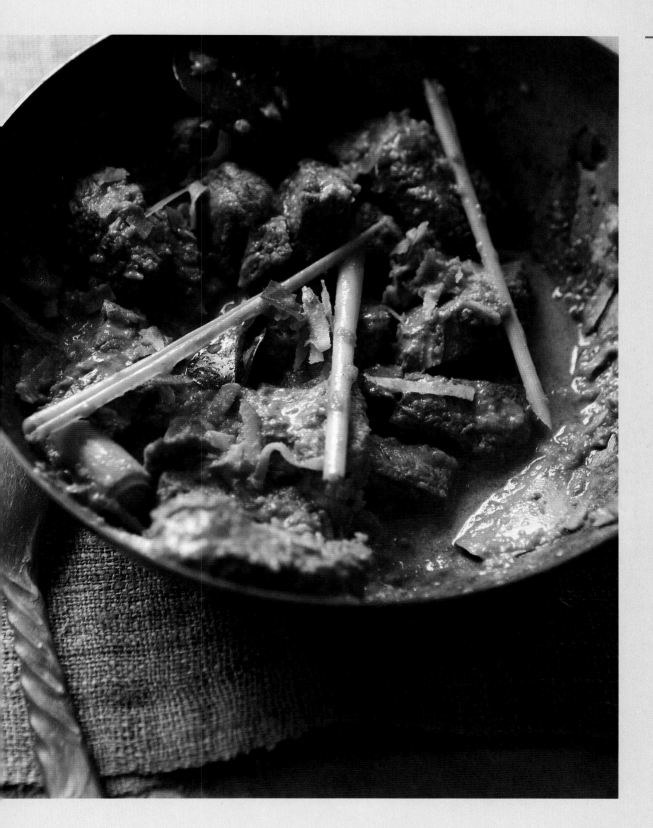

penang assam laksa

Assam Laksa is just one of the many variations of Laksa. You can use lime zest or tamarind peel – asam gelugor or asam keping – to add an extra level of sourness to the broth. The combination of flavours – saltiness, sourness and spiciness is a bold feature and makes Assam Laksa stand out from other variations.

SERVES 4–6
PREPARATION TIME 1 hour
COOKING TIME 45 minutes, plus
cooking the noodles

700g/1lb 9oz whole mackerels
  or herrings, gutted, scaled
  and trimmed by your
  fishmonger
2 stalks Vietnamese coriander
4–5 strips lime zest or
  tamarind peel
1 recipe quantity Assam Laksa
  Spice Paste (*see page 206*)
1 tbsp granulated sugar
4 tbsp lime juice or 2 tbsp lime
  juice and 1 recipe quantity
  Tamarind Water
  (*see page 217*)
500g/1lb 2oz cooked thick rice
  noodles, such as Lai Fun (*see
  page 215*)
sea salt

TOPPINGS
1 small cucumber, halved
  lengthways, deseeded and
  cut into matchsticks
2 wedges fresh pineapple,
  peeled and cut into strips
½ red onion, thinly sliced
1 handful of mint leaves
2–3 green bird's eye chillies,
  deseeded and finely sliced

TO SERVE
1 lime, cut into wedges

1 Rinse the mackerels or herrings inside and out under running cold water and pat dry with kitchen paper. Pour 2 litres/70fl oz/8 cups water into a large saucepan over a high heat and bring to the boil. Add the fish and boil for a few seconds, then reduce the heat to low and cook for about 10 minutes. Remove the herrings from the simmering stock and leave to one side to cool.

2 Put the Vietnamese coriander and lime zest in a spice bag or secure in a piece of muslin and add to the fish stock along with the spice paste, sugar and lime juice. Season with salt and simmer for about 25 minutes.

3 Meanwhile, using a fork, flake the fish, removing the bones and skin. Ten minutes before the end of making the stock, add the fish.

4 When ready to serve, drain the warm, cooked rice noodles and divide into deep soup bowls. Remove the spice bag from the stock and ladle the stock and fish over the noodles. Sprinkle over the topping ingredients and serve warm with lime wedges on the side.

singaporean fish ball noodle soup

SERVES 4–6
PREPARATION TIME 50 minutes, plus making the stock
COOKING TIME 15 minutes

800g/1lb 12oz boneless, skinless white fish fillets, such as pollock or cod
¼ tsp sea salt
4½ tsp cornflour
4 tbsp sunflower oil
6 garlic cloves, finely chopped
150g/5½oz/1¼ cups bean sprouts
350g/12oz cooked 3mm/⅛in or 5mm/¼in rice sticks (*see page 215*)
1 recipe quantity Chicken Stock (*see page 210*)
2 spring onions, finely chopped
freshly ground black pepper

DIPPING SAUCE
1 red chilli, deseeded and sliced
1 tsp lime juice
2 tbsp light soy sauce

1 Cut the fish fillets into bite-sized pieces, then transfer to a food processor. Blend to a rough paste and then transfer to a large bowl. In a separate jug or bowl, mix together the salt, cornflour and 45ml/1½fl oz/3 tablespoons cold water, then slowly stir into the fish paste and mix until well combined. Season with pepper.

2 Prepare a small bowl of water and add a pinch of salt. Moisten one hand in the salted water to avoid the fish paste sticking, gather up the fish paste and shape into a ball. Pick up the ball, then slam it down into the bowl a few times until the mixture is glossy and the texture is smooth and springy. Remoisten your hand as necessary.

3 Use a teaspoon or melon baller to scoop up the fish paste and shape into a ball. It doesn't have to be perfectly round. Place the ball on a plate and continue until all the fish paste has been used. Cover the fish balls with cling film and leave to one side. Meanwhile, to make the dipping sauce, mix together all the ingredients in a small bowl.

4 Heat the oil in a frying pan over a medium heat. Add the garlic and stir-fry for 1–2 minutes until fragrant and starting to brown. Remove the pan from the heat and leave to one side.

5 Bring a saucepan of water to the boil and blanch the bean sprouts for about 20 seconds. Divide the warm, cooked rice sticks into deep soup bowls, then top with the blanched bean sprouts.

6 Pour the chicken stock into a saucepan over a medium-high heat and bring to the boil. Add the fish balls, reduce the heat to low and cook in the simmering stock for 3–4 minutes until they float to the surface. Using a slotted spoon, remove the fish balls from the stock and divide into the bowls of noodles and bean sprouts. Sprinkle over the spring onions and fried garlic, and drizzle over the garlic oil. Bring the chicken stock to a vigorous boil, then ladle it over the noodles. Serve immediately with the dipping sauce on the side.

Drunken Prawns

The name itself gives a not-so-subtle hint that the prawns are cooked in a generous amount of alcohol. Chinese rice wine, Shaoxing, is widely used in Malay cooking, as it enhances flavour and also imparts a very light, earthy fragrance.

SERVES 4
PREPARATION TIME 20 minutes, plus 1 hour 10 minutes marinating and resting time
COOKING TIME 10–15 minutes

500g/1lb 2oz raw, unpeeled large king prawns
3 tbsp Shaoxing rice wine
2 tbsp light soy sauce
2 spring onions, cut into 5cm/2in pieces and thinly sliced lengthways
2.5cm/1in piece of root ginger, peeled and thinly sliced
1 egg, beaten
freshly ground black pepper

TO SERVE
1 recipe quantity Boiled Long-Grain Rice (*see page 214*)

1 Using a pair of kitchen scissors, trim off each prawn the feelers, rostrum, legs and the sharp end of the tail. Make a slit along the back of the prawn with a sharp knife and pull out the black vein with the tip of the knife or your fingers. Rinse the prawns under running cold water and pat dry with kitchen paper.

2 Arrange the prawns on a heatproof dish that will fit inside a wok or an electric steamer, if using. Pour over the rice wine and soy sauce and season with pepper. Cover with cling film and leave to marinate in the fridge for 1 hour. Remove from the fridge and leave to stand at room temperature for about 10 minutes before cooking.

3 Place a round steamer rack with legs at least 2.5cm/1in tall inside a wok. Leaving a minimum gap of 1cm/½in below the steamer, add water to the wok and bring to the boil over a medium-high heat. Sprinkle the spring onions and ginger over the prawns, then set the dish on the rack and cover the wok. Steam for 10–15 minutes until the prawns turn pink and are cooked through. Keep an eye on the level of the water, adding more boiling water if necessary.

4 Two minutes before the end of cooking, pour over the beaten egg. Serve warm with boiled rice.

malaysian prawn fritters & tofu with butternut squash sauce

This Malaysian-style salad is an interesting collaboration of ingredients from different ethnic backgrounds: prawn fritters, known as Cucur Udang in Malay, is a truly authentic Malaysian food; the spices used are typical of those used in Indian cuisine; and the tofu comes from Chinese cuisine. Together, the different flavours and textures combine to make a wonderfully tasty fusion dish.

SERVES 4–6
PREPARATION TIME 45 minutes –1 hour
COOKING TIME 1 hour 30 minutes

150g/5½oz firm tofu, cut into bite-sized cubes
200g/7oz/2 cups mixed sprouts or bean sprouts
1 small cucumber, quartered lengthways, deseeded and cut into matchsticks
200g/7oz Jerusalem artichokes, water chestnuts or jicama, peeled and cut into matchsticks
3 hard-boiled eggs, halved

BUTTERNUT SQUASH SAUCE
200g/7oz butternut squash, deseeded, peeled and cut into bite-sized pieces
100g/3½oz/scant ⅔ cup unsalted macadamia nuts
4 shallots, roughly chopped
2 red chillies, deseeded and roughly chopped
2 tbsp sunflower oil
3 tbsp grated palm sugar or soft light brown sugar
1½ tsp sea salt
1 tbsp lime juice or ½ recipe quantity Tamarind Water (*see page 217*)

1 To make the butternut squash sauce, put the butternut squash in a saucepan of boiling water and cook for 10 minutes, or until tender. Drain, mash until very smooth and leave to one side.

2 Meanwhile, heat a frying pan over a medium-high heat, then add the macadamia nuts and dry-roast until fragrant and starting to brown. Remove from the heat and roughly grind in a food processor or blender – you want a fine powder with some chunky bits.

3 Put the shallots and chillies in a food processor or blender and blend to a smooth paste. Heat the oil in a saucepan over a medium-high heat. Add the chilli paste and cook for 10 minutes, or until fragrant, stirring occasionally.

4 Stir the mashed butternut squash, sugar and salt into the paste, then add the lime juice and 210ml/7½fl oz/generous ¾ cup water. Bring to the boil, then reduce the heat to low and simmer for 5–10 minutes until the sauce starts to thicken, stirring occasionally. Add the ground macadamia nuts and cook for a further 2–3 minutes. Leave to one side and keep warm.

5 To make the batter for the prawn fritters, mix together the flour, turmeric and chilli powder in a large mixing bowl. Season with salt and pepper, then gradually stir in 100ml/3½fl oz/generous ⅓ cup water to form a smooth, thick batter. Add the egg, prawns, spring onions and shallots and leave to one side.

6 Heat the oil in a deep, heavy-based saucepan to 180°C/350°F or until a small piece of bread turns brown in 15 seconds. Gently drop 2 heaped tablespoons of the batter into the oil and fry for 3–4 minutes until golden brown. You can fry several fritters at a time, as long as they are well spaced. Using a slotted spoon, remove the fritters from the oil and drain on kitchen paper. Repeat until all the batter is used, then slice the fritters into chunks and keep warm.

PRAWN FRITTERS

80g/2¾oz/scant ⅔ cup
  self-raising flour
½ tsp turmeric
¼ tsp chilli powder
1 egg, beaten
250g/9oz raw, peeled large
  king prawns, deveined
  (*see page 216*)
2 spring onions, finely
  chopped
3 shallots, thinly sliced
500ml/17fl oz/2 cups
  sunflower oil, for deep-frying
sea salt and freshly ground
  black pepper

7 Bring the oil back to a temperature of 180°C/350°F. Deep-fry the tofu in batches for 3–4 minutes until the tofu is golden brown and crispy. Using a slotted spoon, remove the tofu from the oil and drain on kitchen paper, keeping warm until all the tofu is used.

8 Meanwhile, bring a small saucepan of water to the boil and blanch the mixed sprouts for about 20 seconds and drain.

9 Divide the cucumber, Jerusalem artichokes, mixed sprouts, hard-boiled eggs, tofu and prawn fritters between plates. Ladle over the warm butternut squash sauce and serve immediately.

singaporean CHILLI CraB

This slightly sweet, hot and spicy dish is undoubtedly one of the most popular ways to prepare crabs in Singapore. Fresh, meaty crabs are essential. When choosing a crab, gently press on the underbelly – if it is firm, then it will be more meaty. If using crab claws and not whole crabs, make sure that you crack the shell slightly before cooking, so that the flesh soaks up all the sauce. The shells will also peel away more easily.

SERVES 4
PREPARATION TIME 45 minutes
COOKING TIME 20–25 minutes

1.5kg/3lb 5oz uncooked brown or blue swimmer crabs, or crab claws, scrubbed
3 tbsp sunflower oil
1 recipe quantity Chilli Crab Spice Paste (*see page 206*)
2 tbsp tomato ketchup
2 tbsp chilli sauce
2 tbsp clear honey
3 tbsp light soy sauce

TO SERVE
1 recipe quantity Boiled Long-Grain Rice (*see page 214*)

1 To prepare each crab, pull off the triangular bony tail flap and discard. Press your thumb under the rear end of the crab and lift the body away from the back shell. Discard the shell and remove and discard the stomach bag and the gills at the sides of the body. Rinse the crab flesh and claws under running cold water and pat dry with kitchen paper. Pull the 2 front claws from the bodies and then, using the back of a knife or a mallet, slightly crack the shell of each claw. Cut the crabs into quarters with a large-bladed knife. If using crab claws only, rinse under running cold water and crack the claws slighty using a large-bladed knife.

2 Heat the oil in a wok or large frying pan over a high heat. Add the spice paste and cook gently, stirring occasionally, for 10–15 minutes until fragrant and the oil starts to rise to the surface.

3 Meanwhile, combine the tomato ketchup, chilli sauce, honey and soy sauce in a small bowl. Add the sauce mixture to the wok or pan, then pour in 90ml/3fl oz/generous ⅓ cup water and bring to the boil.

4 Tip in the crab pieces and push around the wok or pan until well coated with the sauce. Cover, reduce the heat to low and simmer for 8–10 minutes until the crab pieces turn bright orange and are cooked through. Serve immediately with boiled rice.

malaysian coconut & lemongrass – scented rice with squid sambal

SERVES 4–6
PREPARATION TIME 1 hour, plus soaking and resting time
COOKING TIME 1 hour 15 minutes

350g/12oz/1¾ cups long-grain rice, washed and rested
1 star anise
2 lemongrass stalks, outer leaves and stalk ends removed and crushed
3 pandan leaves, tied into a knot (optional)
2cm/¾in piece of root ginger, peeled and finely chopped
100ml/3½fl oz/generous ⅓ cup coconut milk
½ tsp sea salt
4–6 banana leaves (optional)

SQUID SAMBAL
4 tbsp sunflower oil
2 red onions, sliced into rings
1 recipe quantity Squid Spice Paste (*see page 209*)
800g/1lb 12oz squid, cut into rings (*see page 216*)
1 tbsp granulated sugar
2 tbsp lime juice or 1 recipe quantity Tamarind Water (*see page 217*)
sea salt

TO SERVE
100g/3½oz/scant ⅔ cup raw, skinless peanuts
1 tsp granulated sugar
2 hard-boiled eggs, quartered
1 small cucumber, halved lengthways, deseeded and cut into chunks
80g/2¾oz toasted dried anchovies (*see page 217*)

1 To make the Squid Sambal, heat the oil in a frying pan over a medium-high heat, then add the onions and cook until soft and translucent. Add the spice paste and cook gently, stirring occasionally, for 10–15 minutes until fragrant and the oil starts to rise to the surface. Tip in the squid, stir until well coated and cook for about 5 minutes. Add the sugar and season with salt, then add the lime juice and stir to combine. Bring to the boil, then reduce the heat to low and simmer, covered, for 45 minutes, or until the sauce thickens and turns a dark reddish brown. Leave to one side and keep warm.

2 Meanwhile, put the rice, star anise, lemongrass, pandan leaves, if using, ginger, coconut milk and salt in a large saucepan and pour in 300ml/10½fl oz/scant 1¼ cups water. Put the pan over a high heat and bring to the boil for about 20 seconds. Stir with a wooden spoon to prevent the rice sticking to the base of the pan, reduce the heat to low, cover, and simmer gently for 20 minutes.

3 Remove the pan from the heat, leaving the lid tightly closed, and leave to one side to steam for 10–15 minutes until cooked. Fluff the rice with a fork and discard the star anise, lemongrass and pandan leaves, if using. Leave to one side and keep warm.

4 While the Sambal and rice are cooking, heat a frying pan over a medium-high heat, then add the peanuts and dry-roast until fragrant and starting to brown. Tip the peanuts onto a plate, sprinkle over the sugar and leave to cool.

5 Serve the rice on plates or banana leaves. Ladle the Squid Sambal over the rice and top with the eggs. To the side, heap the cucumber, toasted anchovies and sugared peanuts. Serve hot.

roti canai with dahl curry

Roti Canai, also known as Roti Prata, is served at mamak stalls – the al fresco hawker places you find almost everywhere in Kuala Lumpur. They are normally made by flipping the dough in the air and flapping it on the work surface until it is very thin – a fantastic sight. While you might like to try this technique at home, here I suggest you rest the dough on the work surface and stretch it out as thinly as you can without it tearing.

SERVES 4–6
PREPARATION TIME 1 hour, plus minimum 7 hours resting time
COOKING TIME 1 hour 40 minutes–2 hours

1 tsp sea salt
1 egg
4½ tsp condensed milk
1 tbsp butter, melted
500g/1lb 2oz/4 cups plain flour, plus extra for dusting
55ml/1¾fl oz/scant ¼ cup sunflower oil, plus extra for brushing and kneading

DAHL CURRY
1 tbsp sunflower oil
3 sprigs of curry leaves, rinsed
2 dried chillies, rinsed
1 onion, roughly chopped
2 carrots, diced
1 tbsp garam masala
½ tsp ground ginger
1 tsp turmeric
1 tbsp tomato purée
3 tomatoes, skinned and roughly chopped (*see page 217*)
250g/9oz drained, tinned lentils or 120g/4¼oz/scant ⅔ cup green lentils, soaked overnight
sea salt and freshly ground black pepper

1 Mix the salt together with 190ml/6½fl oz/generous ¾ cup water in a small bowl and set aside. In a separate bowl, mix together the egg, condensed milk and melted butter until well combined. Put the flour into a large mixing bowl and make a well in the centre. Slowly pour in the egg mixture and combine with the flour to form a soft dough. Cover with cling film and leave at room temperature for about 30 minutes.

2 Turn the dough out onto a lightly floured surface and knead for 5 minutes until it is smooth and elastic. Flatten the dough and split in half. Divide each half into 4–5 equal portions and roll each piece into a ball. Brush the dough balls generously with oil, then place side by side on a well-oiled dish. Sprinkle over more oil, about 55ml/1¾fl oz/scant ¼ cup, and cover with cling film. Leave to rest at room temperature for at least 6 hours, or for the best result, overnight.

3 Oil a clean working surface and generously oil your palms. Take a dough ball and flatten, then slowly work the dough outwards from around the edge to expand it, then use your fingers to slowly pull around the edge of the dough to stretch it out. Do this carefully so as not to tear the pastry. Continue until the dough is very thin and almost translucent. Sprinkle some oil over the pastry and fold the edges into the centre to form a square. Air will be trapped as you fold, which will help make the roti crispy and fluffy once cooked. Set aside on an oiled dish and continue until all the dough balls are used. Leave to rest for 20 minutes.

4 Heat a ridged griddle pan over a high heat. When hot, add a roti and cook for 5–6 minutes on each side until blisters and brown spots form. Remove from the pan to a clean surface and, using your hands, gently whack it a few times moving in a circle around the roti to fluff it up. Keep warm and repeat until all the dough balls are used. Meanwhile cook the dahl.

5 To make the dahl, heat the oil in a frying pan over a medium-high heat, then add the curry leaves and dried chillies and stir-fry until fragrant. Add the onion and stir-fry for 1–2 minutes until softened, then add the carrots and cook for 4–5 minutes until the carrots are tender, stirring occasionally. Add the garam masala, ginger, turmeric and tomato purée and stir to combine.

6 Tip in the tomatoes and lentils, then pour in 350ml/12fl oz/scant 1½ cups water. Bring to the boil for about 20 seconds, season with salt and pepper and then reduce the heat to low and cover. If using tinned lentils simmer for 10–15 minutes and if using soaked lentils simmer for 30–45 minutes, or until the dhal is very soft, stirring occasionally. Serve the roti warm with the hot dhal curry.

Nyonya pineapple curry

Pajeri Nanas, cooked the Nyonya way, simmers in a bright red, chilli-based sauce. An alternative way to make this dish is to use curry powder, but you miss out on the pureness of the fresh spices against the natural sweetness of the pineapple. Eaten with fluffy white rice, this aromatic dish with its slight hint of spiciness and natural sweetness of the pineapple seems like pure indulgence.

SERVES 4
PREPARATION TIME 30 minutes
COOKING TIME 40 minutes

1 ripe pineapple
1 tbsp sea salt
3 tbsp sunflower oil
2 star anise
6cm/2½in cinnamon stick
4 cloves
3 green cardamom pods
1 recipe quantity Pajeri Nanas
  Spice Paste (*see page 208*)
1–2 tbsp grated palm sugar or
  soft light brown sugar
30g/1oz/¼ cup dried
  cranberries, dried sour
  cherries, sultanas or raisins
sea salt

TO SERVE
1 recipe quantity Boiled
  Long-Grain Rice (*see page 214*)

1 Cut the crown, about 2cm/¾in from the end, and the base off the pineapple, then, with the pineapple upright, carefully slice off the skin. Don't slice too deeply to remove the 'eyes', as good, edible flesh will be wasted. The 'eyes' on the pineapple run neatly in a spiral around the pineapple. To cut these out, place the pineapple horizontally and position a knife at an angle alongside 3 or 4 'eyes'. Cut a V-shape around the 'eyes', remove them and discard. Repeat, following the spiral, until all 'eyes' are removed.

2 Rub the salt into the pineapple all round, then rinse under running cold water and pat dry with kitchen paper. This is to take away the acidity of the pineapple. Place the pineapple horizontally on a chopping board and cut it into 1cm/½in slices, then use a small ring cutter to remove the core from each piece. Leave the rings to one side and discard the cores.

3 Heat the oil in a large saucepan over a medium heat. Add the star anise, cinnamon stick, cloves and cardamom pods and cook for 3–4 minutes until fragrant, stirring occasionally. Add the spice paste and cook gently, stirring occasionally, for 10–15 minutes until fragrant and the oil starts to rise to the surface.

4 Add the pineapple slices and push around the pan with a wooden spoon until the pineapple is well coated with the paste. Pour in 170ml/5½fl oz/⅔ cup water and bring to the boil for about 20 seconds, then add the sugar and season with salt. Reduce the heat to low and simmer, covered, for 15 minutes until the pineapple is soft and the liquid starts to thicken.

5 Sprinkle the dried cranberries into the pan, cover and simmer for a further 2–3 minutes. Adjust the sweetness or sourness by adding a touch of salt and sugar, as required. Serve warm with boiled rice.

CRISPY PORK ROLLS

The ingredient that makes these rolls something really special is bean curd skin. There are two types available – one is opaque and a medium-yellow colour and the other is translucent and slightly oiled. Either bean curd is fine to use and can be found in most Asian supermarkets. If you cannot get bean curd skin, they are also delicious when made with Chinese spring roll wrappers, which are also known as egg roll wrappers.

MAKES 12 rolls
PREPARATION TIME 1 hour, plus 1 hour 20 minutes marinating, resting and cooling time
COOKING TIME 25 minutes

1 x 500g/1lb 2oz pork tenderloin
2 tbsp sesame oil
1 tsp five-spice powder
2 tsp clear honey
1 tbsp light soy sauce
¼ tsp ground pepper
1 tbsp sesame seeds
2 tbsp cornflour
8 shallots, finely sliced
1 bean curd skin, wiped with a damp tea towel or 12 Chinese spring roll wrappers, about 16 x 18cm/6¼ x 7in in size
500ml/17fl oz/2 cups sunflower oil, for deep-frying

TO SERVE
mint, Thai basil and coriander leaf salad (optional)

1 Place the pork horizontally on a chopping board, then use a paring knife or a flexible, fine-bladed knife to trim off any fat and silver skin. To trim off the silver skin, slip the knife between the meat and the skin and slide the knife along the length of the tenderloin. Slice the pork into 5–10mm/¼–½in strips and put into a bowl.

2 Put the sesame oil, five-spice powder, honey, soy sauce, ground pepper, sesame seeds, cornflour and shallots in with the pork, then toss until the pieces of pork are well coated. Cover with cling film and leave to marinate in the fridge for 1 hour.

3 Remove the pork from the fridge and leave to stand at room temperature for about 10 minutes before making the rolls. Meanwhile, lay the bean curd skin, if using, on a chopping board and cut into twelve 16 x 18cm/6¼ x 7in sheets.

4 Place 4 or 5 strips of the marinated pork horizontally along the centre of a bean curd sheet or spring roll wrapper, leaving a gap of about 1cm/½in around the edges. Fold the bottom edge over the filling, then fold in the two sides and roll up tightly. Lightly moisten the upper edge to seal, then place on a plate, cover with a damp tea towel and repeat until all the ingredients are used.

5 Place the pork rolls on a plate and place in a bamboo or electric steamer and steam for 8–10 minutes until firm to the touch. Remove from the steamer and leave for about 10 minutes to cool slightly.

6 Heat the oil in a deep, heavy-based saucepan to 180°C/350°F or until a small piece of bread turns brown in 15 seconds. Gently slide 4 or 5 pork rolls into the oil and fry for 5 minutes, or until the pork rolls are golden brown. Drain the rolls on kitchen paper and keep warm while you fry the remaining pork rolls.

7 Cut the rolls into 2cm/¾in pieces and serve hot with a herb leaf salad, if you like.

malay-style madeleines with coconut, lime & chocolate

Whenever the festive season is around the corner, whether it's Chinese New Year or Eid Mubarak, these little cakes are baked in most households. The texture is light and fluffy and they resemble French Madeleines. These are traditionally made using specific moulds of many different and beautiful shapes, such as flowers, fish and sea shells, but a mini muffin mould or Madeleine mould can also be used. I have given a little bit of a modern twist by adding desiccated coconut, a touch of lime and some chocolate sprinkles.

SERVES 4
PREPARATION TIME 10 minutes
COOKING TIME 30 minutes

melted butter, for greasing
4 eggs
90g/3¼oz/heaped ⅓ cup
    caster sugar
¼ tsp baking powder
100g/3½oz/ heaped ¾ cup
    plain flour
1 tbsp lime juice
zest of 1 lime
3 tbsp desiccated coconut
2 tbsp chocolate sprinkles

1 Preheat the oven to 200°C/°F/Gas 6 and lightly grease a Madeleine or mini muffin mould with melted butter.
2 Using an electric mixer, beat the eggs and sugar together in a large mixing bowl and beat until thick and creamy. Add the baking powder and gradually fold in the flour using a spatula.
3 Add the lime juice, lime zest, desiccated coconut and chocolate sprinkles and gently fold through using a spatula.
4 Spoon the mixture into the prepared mould until each cup is three-quarters full. Put in the preheated oven and bake for about 7–8 minutes, or until golden brown. Remove from the oven and turn the madeleines out of the tin onto a wire cooling rack. Grease the mould again and repeat with the remaining batter and leave to cool completely.

sago pearls with coconut & chocolate syrup

I love coconut milk with an added hint of saltiness, and this Malay dessert, of Peranakan Chinese origin, is a fantastic example of how well the sweet and salty combination works. Here you also have the combination of palm sugar and coconut milk, which provide big flavours in a very simple way.

SERVES 4–6
PREPARATION TIME 20 minutes, plus 1 hour chilling
COOKING TIME 55 minutes

300g/10½oz/scant 1⅔ cups small sago pearls
1 vanilla pod
200ml/7fl oz/scant ¾ cup + 2 tbsp coconut milk
200g/7oz/heaped 1 cup palm sugar, grated, or soft light brown sugar
1 tsp unsweetened cocoa powder
sea salt

1 Bring a large saucepan of water to the boil. Add the sago pearls, reduce the heat to medium-low and cook, uncovered, for 30 minutes, or until they become translucent, stirring occasionally to stop the pearls from sticking. Add more boiling water if the sago gets too sticky. Drain in a colander and rinse under running cold water, lightly rubbing the sago to wash away the starch.

2 Divide the sago pearls into 4-6 100ml/3½fl oz/generous ⅓ cup ramekins. Press down on the sago to level the surface and make compact. Cover with cling film and chill in the fridge for 1 hour.

3 Meanwhile, split the vanilla pod in two, using a small sharp knife, and scrape the seeds into a small saucepan. Add the coconut milk, season generously with salt and place over a medium heat. Slowly bring to the boil, stirring constantly. When bubbles start to form, remove from the heat and strain through a fine sieve into a bowl. Leave to one side to cool.

4 Put the sugar, cocoa powder and 90ml/3fl oz/⅓ cup + 1 tablespoon water into a separate small saucepan over a medium heat. Slowly dissolve the sugar, stirring constantly, until it becomes syrupy. Leave to one side.

5 When the sago is set and chilled, turn the sago out onto individual serving plates. Drizzle over the cocoa sugar syrup and then the coconut milk. Serve slightly chilled.

THAILAND

Thailand is a land abundant with fresh produce, dried spices and fresh aromatic herbs and roots. The Thai are a warm and smiling people who firmly believe in how food can bond people. They love to eat and it is because of their passion for food that there are so many amazing dishes to choose from.

Essential ingredients in Thai cooking are fish sauce and dried shrimps, which bring pungency and saltiness to dishes, and are the main components of the often-used flavouring Nam Prik Pao (*see page 212*); bird's eye chillies to add spiciness; tamarind and lime for a delicious sourness; and fresh and fragrant lemongrass, kaffir lime leaves and galangal. Prawn Tom Yum Soup (*see page 135*), sharp in taste with a pleasant chilli kick, is a mouth-watering dish that uses all of these to create perfect harmony.

Other ingredients that are symbolic of Thai cuisine are coconut milk, coriander roots and Thai basil, providing the key flavours in the ubiquitous Thai Green Chicken Curry (*see page 124*), and palm sugar, which delicately balances the sour notes in many Thai dishes, including the superbly refreshing noodle-based dishes Phuket-Style Pad Thai (*see page 132*) and Green Papaya Salad (*see page 139*).

Rice is Thailand's staple food and every meal is based around it. Cellophane or rice noodles are also very popular and they are usually served in a soup or stir-fry – Chiang Mai Curry Noodle Soup (*see page 122*) is an immediately popular example.

cнiang mai curry noodle soup

This curry noodle dish is from north Thailand and takes on influences from its neighbouring country, Burma. One of these is the deep-fried egg noodles, which add a crunchy texture.

SERVES 4–6
PREPARATION TIME 30 minutes
COOKING TIME 40–45 minutes

250ml/9fl oz/1 cup sunflower oil
1 recipe quantity Thai Red Curry Spice Paste (*see page 210*)
800g/1lb 12oz skinless, boneless chicken thighs, cut into bite-sized pieces
500ml/17fl oz/2 cups coconut milk
3 tbsp fish sauce
1 tsp grated palm sugar or soft light brown sugar
300g/10½oz dried fine egg noodles
200g/7oz dried rice vermicelli
1 handful of coriander leaves, to serve

TO SERVE
1 lime, cut into wedges

1 Heat 1 tablespoon of the oil in a large saucepan over a medium-high heat. Add the spice paste and cook gently, stirring occasionally, for 10–15 minutes until fragrant and the oil starts to rise to the surface. Add the chicken and toss until each piece of chicken is well coated in the paste, then cook, stirring occasionally, for 8–10 minutes until the chicken starts to turn golden brown.

2 Add half of the coconut milk and gently boil for 5–7 minutes until the coconut milk starts to thicken, then add the remaining coconut milk and 1 litre/35fl oz/4 cups water. Push the chicken around the pan until well coated with the sauce. Add the fish sauce and sugar and cook for a further 10 minutes, or until the chicken is cooked through.

3 Meanwhile, heat the remaining oil in a deep, heavy-based saucepan to 170°C/325°F or until a small piece of bread turns brown in 20 seconds. Take 50g/1¾oz of the egg noodles and separate the strands. Fry the strands in small batches until golden brown all round and leave to one side.

4 Prepare a large bowl of ice-cold water and place it next to the hob. Fill a large saucepan with plenty of water and bring to the boil, then add the remaining egg noodles and cook for 3–4 minutes. Using a noodle skimmer or kitchen tongs, remove the noodles from the water and plunge for a few seconds into the cold water, meanwhile bringing the water in the pan back to the boil. Return the noodles to the pan for a few seconds to warm through, then drain and divide the noodles into bowls. Use the same process to cook the dried vermicelli, except cook for 2–3 minutes.

5 Add the chicken pieces and hot curry broth. Top with the fried egg noodles, sprinkle over the coriander and serve with lime wedges on the side.

THAI green CHICKen curry

My introduction to Thai Green Chicken Curry was as a teenager, and as my interest in this fresh-flavoured curry grew I learnt to make green curry paste from scratch, and have discovered that the most important ingredient is coriander root because of its intense flavour. If you cannot find coriander root, use the coriander leaves and stalks instead.

SERVES 4
PREPARATION TIME 30 minutes
COOKING TIME 40 minutes

500g/1lb 2oz chicken
  drumsticks or skinless
  chicken thighs
2 tsp sunflower oil
1 recipe quantity Thai Green
  Curry Spice Paste (*see page
  210*)
3 kaffir lime leaves
200ml/7fl oz/scant 1 cup thick
  coconut milk
100g/3½oz pea aubergines
6 apple aubergines, cut in half
2 tbsp fish sauce
50g/1¾oz of Thai basil leaves

TO SERVE
1 recipe quantity Boiled
  Long-Grain Rice (*see page
  214 – optional*)

1 If using chicken drumsticks, rinse them under running cold water and pat dry with kitchen paper. Remove the skin and then, using a sharp cleaver or large chef's knife, cut each drumstick into 2 pieces through the bone. Remove the knuckles with a pair of kitchen scissors.

2 Heat the oil in a large saucepan over a medium-high heat. Add the spice paste and cook gently, stirring occasionally, for 10–15 minutes, until fragrant and the oil starts to rise to the surface. Add the kaffir lime leaves and chicken pieces and toss the chicken until well coated with the paste, then cook, stirring occasionally, for 5–6 minutes until starting to turn golden brown.

3 Add the coconut milk to the pan and bring to the boil, then add the pea and apple aubergines and fish sauce. Reduce the heat to low and simmer for 20–25 minutes until the sauce starts to thicken, the chicken is cooked through and the aubergines are soft. Carefully scoop off any oil as it forms on the surface. Stir in the Thai basil and serve warm with boiled rice, if you like.

THAI ROAST CHICKEN

This Thai-style roast chicken, Gai Yaang, is a very popular Thai street food. During my first visit to southern Thailand, when I was young, I remember visiting one particular market, and still remember the aromas of the Gai Yaang. Traditionally, this dish is cooked over a charcoal grill and is served with rice or Green Papaya Salad (*see page 139*).

SERVES 4
PREPARATION TIME 30 minutes, plus minimum 6 hours 30 minutes marinating and resting time
COOKING TIME 45 minutes–1 hour

1 x 1.5kg/3lb 5oz whole chicken
1 tbsp sea salt
1 recipe quantity Thai Roast Chicken Spice Paste (*see page 210*)
2 tbsp fish sauce
1 tbsp clear honey

TO SERVE
Green Papaya Salad (*see page 139*)

1 Remove the neck, gizzards and fat from inside the chicken. Rinse the chicken thoroughly inside and out under running cold water. Lightly rub the salt onto the skin, then rinse the chicken again and pat dry with kitchen paper. To spatchcock the chicken, place it breast-side down on a chopping board and then, using a pair of kitchen scissors, cut off the tail and cut along each side of the backbone, discarding the bone. Turn the chicken over and press down on the breast to slightly flatten the chicken.

2 Mix together the spice paste, fish sauce and honey in a large bowl, then add the chicken and thoroughly coat all round with the mixture. Transfer to a plate, cover with cling film and leave to marinate in the fridge for 6 hours or, for and even better flavour, overnight.

3 Remove the chicken from the fridge and leave to stand at room temperature for 30 minutes before cooking. Preheat the oven to 180°C/350°F/Gas 4. Put the chicken on a baking tray and bake for 45 minutes–1 hour until golden and cooked through. When the tip of a sharp knife is inserted into the thickest part of the meat, the juices should run clear. Remove from the oven and leave to rest for 5 minutes.

4 To serve, cut the chicken in half through the breast. Take one side of the chicken and, using a sharp knife, cut through the bone to remove the thigh and drumstick whole. Cut through the joint to remove the wing, then cut the breast into 4 chunky pieces. Repeat the same steps to cut up the other half of the chicken. Serve hot with the Green Papaya Salad.

spicy chicken & pine nut stir-fry

SERVES 4
PREPARATION TIME 20 minutes
COOKING TIME 20 minutes

100g/3½oz/⅔ cup pine nuts
2 tbsp sunflower oil
500g/1lb 2oz boneless,
  skinless chicken breasts, cut
  into bite-sized pieces
1 red onion, cut into wedges
4 garlic cloves, finely chopped
4 dried chillies, deseeded,
  soaked and roughly chopped
2 tsp Nam Prik Pao (*see page
  212*)
2 tsp fish sauce
1 tsp clear honey
2 spring onions, cut
  lengthways into 5cm/2in
  pieces
1 recipe quantity Boiled
  Long-Grain Rice, to serve
  (*see page 214*)

1 Heat a frying pan over a medium-high heat, then add the pine nuts and dry-roast until fragrant and starting to brown. Leave to one side.

2 Add 1 tablespoon of the oil to the frying pan and when the oil is hot, add the chicken pieces and stir-fry for 1–2 minutes until sealed. Using a slotted spoon, remove the chicken from the pan, drain on kitchen paper and leave to one side.

3 Clean the pan, then heat the remaining tablespoon of oil over a medium-high heat. Add the onion, garlic and dried chillies and stir-fry for 2–3 minutes until the onion starts to soften. Add the Nam Prik Pao and stir-fry for 1 minute, then toss through the seared chicken and pine nuts. Add the fish sauce and honey and cook, stirring occasionally, for about 6 minutes, or until the chicken is golden and cooked through. Add in the spring onions and stir-fry for 1 minute before serving immediately with boiled rice.

chilli & thai basil pork

SERVES 4
PREPARATION TIME 25 minutes
COOKING TIME 20 minutes

1 tbsp sunflower oil
5 garlic cloves, finely chopped
500g/1lb 2oz pork mince
2 tsp Nam Prik Pao (*see page
  212*)
1 tsp oyster sauce
2 tsp fish sauce
1 tsp grated palm sugar or soft
  light brown sugar
1 handful of Thai basil leaves
1 recipe quantity Boiled
  Long-Grain Rice, to serve
  (*see page 214*)

1 Heat the oil in a wok over a medium-high heat. Add the garlic and stir-fry for 1–2 minutes until fragrant. Tip in the pork mince, break up the lumps and cook, stirring occasionally, for 5 minutes.

2 Stir in the Nam Prik Pao, oyster sauce, fish sauce and sugar and add 100ml/3½fl oz/generous ⅓ cup water. Bring to the boil, then reduce the heat to medium and cook, stirring occasionally, for 4–5 minutes until the pork mince is cooked. Add the Thai basil leaves, toss for a few seconds and serve immediately with boiled rice.

THAI FRIED RICE WITH PORK & MANGO SALAD

I discovered this recipe by accident at a roadside stall run by a Malay-Thai family. This dish was one of their specialities – Thai-style fried rice topped with well-flavoured pork mince and mango salad served with a small portion of Sambal. The taste combination is amazing, and this dish is comfort food at its best. Mix everything together and tuck in.

SERVES 4–6
PREPARATION TIME 30 minutes, plus 5–10 minutes soaking time and cooking and chilling the rice
COOKING TIME 20 minutes

25g/1oz dried shrimps
2 tbsp sunflower oil
250g/9oz pork mince
3 garlic cloves, finely chopped
1 tbsp chopped coriander stems and leaves
1 recipe quantity Boiled Long-Grain Rice, cooked and chilled for 12 hours or overnight (*see page 214*)
1 tbsp Nam Prik Pao (*see page 212*)
2 tbsp fish sauce
1 tbsp dark soy sauce
Sambal (*see page 213*), to serve

MANGO SALAD
250g/9oz green mango
2 shallots, thinly sliced
2 red bird's eye chillies, deseeded and chopped
2 tbsp fish sauce
2 tbsp lime juice
2 tbsp grated palm sugar or soft light brown sugar
1 handful of mint leaves, roughly chopped
1 handful of coriander leaves, roughly chopped

1 Put the dried shrimps in a small bowl, cover with water and leave to soak for 5–10 minutes. Drain and squeeze out any excess water, pat dry with kitchen paper and then roughly chop and leave to one side.

2 Meanwhile, to make the mango salad, peel the green mango with a potato peeler, then either use a mandolin or zigzag peeler to shred the flesh, leaving behind the flesh nearest the seed. Put the shredded mango in a bowl of cold salted water for 1–2 minutes to draw out the acidity. Drain, pat dry with kitchen paper and transfer to a bowl.

3 Put the shallots and chillies in a mortar and lightly bruise them using a pestle. Alternatively, place on a chopping board and bruise with the flat of a knife blade. Put the minced shallots and chillies in a food processor with the fish sauce, lime juice and sugar and blend until the sugar is dissolved. Pour the mixture over the shredded mango, add the mint and coriander and toss to mix through. Set aside.

4 Heat 1 tablespoon of the oil in a frying pan over a high heat. Tip in the pork mince, break up the lumps and stir-fry for 2 minutes. Stir in the garlic and coriander and cook, stirring occasionally, for 4–5 minutes until the pork is cooked through. Remove from the heat and keep warm.

5 Heat the remaining tablespoon of oil in a wok or frying pan over a high heat until smoking hot. Add the prepared shrimps and cook for 1–2 minutes until fragrant. Tip in the cooked rice, break up any clumps and stir-fry for 2–3 minutes. Add the nam prik pao, fish sauce and soy sauce and stir to combine, and cook for a further 4–5 minutes until heated through. Divide the fried rice onto plates, spoon the pork on top and then sprinkle over the mango salad. Serve hot with the mango salad and Sambal.

beef panang curry

Rich, sweet and creamy with a dark red undertone, this is a lovely comfort dish. In comparison to the ever famous green curry, Panang Curry gives a different dimension with the touch of roasted peanuts. The name of this curry is derived from Penang, an island off the northwest coast of Malaysia. Beef is the popular type of meat to use, however, pork or chicken can also be used and are delicious.

SERVES 4
PREPARATION TIME 15 minutes
COOKING TIME 35–45 minutes

1 x 500g/1lb 2oz beef fillet
400ml/14fl oz/generous
   1½ cups coconut milk
1 recipe quantity Panang
   Curry Spice Paste (*see page 208*)
2 kaffir lime leaves, thinly
   sliced
50g/1¾oz/⅓ cup skinless raw
   peanuts
2 tbsp fish sauce
1 tbsp clear honey
Thai basil leaves, to serve

TO SERVE
1 recipe quantity Boiled
   Long-Grain Rice
   (*see page 214*)

1 Put the beef fillet on a chopping board and then, using a sharp knife, cut against the grain into 5mm/¼in slices and leave to one side.

2 Pour half of the coconut milk into a large saucepan over a medium-high heat and bring to a gentle boil. Add the spice paste and cook, stirring occasionally, for 4–5 minutes until the paste starts to thicken. Add the remaining coconut milk and kaffir lime leaves and cook, stirring occasionally, for a further 3–4 minutes until fragrant and the oil starts to rise to the surface.

3 Meanwhile, heat a frying pan over a medium-high heat, then add the peanuts and dry-roast until fragrant and starting to brown. Remove from the heat and roughly chop.

4 Tip the beef slices into the pan and push around until well coated with the sauce. Cook for a further 4–5 minutes, then stir in the fish sauce and honey. Reduce the heat to low and simmer, covered, for 10–15 minutes until the meat is tender. Five minutes before the end of cooking, stir in the roasted peanuts. Sprinkle over the Thai basil and serve immediately with boiled rice.

PHUKET-STYLE PAD THAI

Pad Thai is one of Thailand's much-loved national dishes that is sold from street carts on most street corners. This Phuket-Style Pad Thai is unique, as it is served on an omelette instead of mixing the shredded omelette into the noodles.

SERVES 4
PREPARATION TIME 20 minutes
COOKING TIME about
  30 minutes, plus cooking the rice
  sticks

2 tbsp sunflower oil, plus extra
  for frying
5 eggs, beaten
50g/1¾oz/⅓ cup skinless raw
  peanuts
60g/2¼oz firm tofu, cut into
  strips
3 garlic cloves, finely chopped
250g/9oz raw, peeled large
  king prawns, deveined
  (*see page 216*)
3 tbsp fish sauce
1 tbsp dark soy sauce
2 tsp Nam Prik Pao (*see page
  212*)
2 tbsp lime juice
2 tsp grated palm sugar or soft
  light brown sugar
300g/10½oz cooked
  5mm/¼in rice sticks
  (*see page 215*)
150g/5½oz/1¼ cups bean
  sprouts
3 spring onions or Chinese
  chives, cut lengthways into
  5cm/2in pieces
1 handful of coriander leaves,
  to serve

1 Heat 1 tablespoon of the oil in a 20cm/8in frying pan over a medium heat. Pour one-quarter of the beaten eggs into the pan and swirl around to evenly coat the base. Cook for 2–3 minutes until the surface starts to set. Using a spatula, turn the omelette over and cook on the other side for 2–3 minutes until cooked through. Slide the omelette onto a plate, then repeat with the remaining egg to make 4 omelettes, adding more oil to the pan if necessary.

2 Meanwhile, heat a frying pan over a medium-high heat, then add the peanuts and dry-roast until fragrant and starting to brown. Remove from the heat and roughly grind the peanuts in a food processor or blender – you want a fine powder with some chunky bits.

3 Heat the remaining 1 tablespoon of oil in a wok or large frying pan over a medium-high heat. Add the tofu and stir-fry for 8–10 minutes until lightly golden brown, then add the garlic and stir-fry for 1–2 minutes until fragrant. Tip in the prawns and cook, stirring occasionally, for 3–4 minutes until they turn pink and are cooked through. Meanwhile, mix the fish sauce, soy sauce, nam prik pao, lime juice and sugar in a small bowl until the sugar is dissolved.

4 Drain the cooked rice sticks, refresh under running cold water and pat dry with kitchen paper. Add the sticks to the wok with the prawns and toss until well combined, then pour over the sauce mixture. Push the ingredients around the pan until well combined, then add 3–4 tablespoons water and stir-fry for 2–3 minutes. Toss through the bean sprouts and spring onions and cook for 1 minute, or until heated through.

5 Put an omelette on each dish, then divide the Pad Thai over the omelettes and sprinkle over the roasted peanuts and coriander. Serve hot.

prawn Tom yum soup

Hot, sour, sweet and salty – these words sum up perfectly this irresistible bowl of Tom Yum Goong. Its distinct flavours are the result of infusing the stock with ginger or galangal as well as fresh lemongrass and kaffir lime leaves, which give a zesty hint of citrus. As an alternative, use chicken thighs or breast instead of the prawns.

SERVES 4–6
PREPARATION TIME 30 minutes,
plus making the stock
COOKING TIME 20 minutes

16 raw, unpeeled large king
  prawns
½ recipe quantity Chicken
  Stock (*see page 210*)
3 lemongrass stalks, outer
  leaves and stalk ends
  removed, crushed and cut
  into 5cm/2in pieces
6 kaffir lime leaves, bruised
5 shallots, peeled and crushed
6–8 red bird's eye chillies,
  whole and slightly bruised
2cm/¾in piece of root ginger
  or galangal, peeled and sliced
200g/7oz oyster mushrooms
  or button mushrooms
2 tbsp Nam Prik Pao (*see page
  212*)
2 tbsp fish sauce
7 tbsp lime juice
2 tsp grated palm sugar or soft
  light brown sugar
½ tsp sea salt
2 tomatoes, skinned and cut
  into quarters (*see page 217*)
1 handful of coriander leaves,
  to serve

1 Using a pair of kitchen scissors, trim off each prawn the feelers, rostrum, legs and the sharp end of the tail. Make a slit along the back of the prawn with a sharp knife and pull out the black vein with the tip of the knife or your fingers. Rinse the prawns under running cold water and pat dry with kitchen paper.

2 Pour the chicken stock into a large saucepan and bring to the boil over a medium-high heat. Add the lemongrass, kaffir lime leaves, shallots, chillies and ginger and cook for 5 minutes, or until fragrant. Add the prawns to the pan, cover and bring back to the boil. Reduce the heat to low and cook for 5–7 minutes until the prawns turn pink and are cooked through.

3 Add the mushrooms to the pan and cook for 2 minutes, then stir in the nam prik pao, fish sauce, lime juice, sugar and salt. The broth should taste sour, slightly salty and sweet. Add more lime juice, if you like. Tip in the tomatoes, bring back to the boil, then remove the pan from the heat.

4 Discard the lemongrass, kaffir lime leaves, shallots and ginger, and serve immediately with the coriander sprinkled over.

spicy steamed squid

SERVES 4
PREPARATION TIME 30 minutes
COOKING TIME 5–7 minutes

500g/1lb 2oz squid, cut into
  rings and tentacles into
  pieces (*see page 216*)
10 cherry tomatoes, halved
1 handful of coriander leaves

DRESSING
2 green bird's eye chillies,
  deseeded and finely chopped
1 red chilli, deseeded and
  finely chopped
2 tbsp fish sauce
3 tbsp lime juice
1 tbsp grated palm sugar or
  soft light brown sugar

1 Combine all the dressing ingredients in a bowl, stirring until the
sugar is dissolved. Place the squid on a plate and place in a bamboo
or electric steamer and steam the squid for 5–7 minutes until it
starts to curl up around the edges and is cooked through.

2 Remove the squid from the steamer and leave to stand at room
temperature for 5 minutes, then transfer to a bowl. Toss through
the cherry tomatoes and coriander, then pour over the dressing.
Serve at room temperature.

prawn & water spinach stir-fry

SERVES 4
PREPARATION TIME 15 minutes
COOKING TIME 10–15 minutes

1 tbsp sunflower oil
2 garlic cloves, finely chopped
200g/7oz raw, peeled large
  king prawns, deveined
  (*see page 216*)
1 tbsp Nam Prik Pao
  (*see page 212*)
400g/14oz water spinach or
  baby leaf spinach
1 tsp fish sauce

1 Heat the oil in a frying pan over a medium-high heat, then add
the garlic and cook for 1–2 minutes until fragrant. Add the prawns
and stir-fry for 5 minutes, or until they turn pink and are cooked
through, then add the nam prik pao and cook for 1 minute.

2 Add the spinach, toss to combine and then cook for 3–4 minutes
if using water spinach, and 1 minute if using baby spinach, or until
the spinach starts to wilt. Add the fish sauce and 3 tablespoons
water, stirring until well combined. Serve immediately.

green papaya salad

A wonderfully simple dish with sweet, sour, spicy and slightly salty flavours. If you can't find green papaya, substitute it with green mango, which usually can be found at Chinese supermarkets. Green mango can be a bit sour compared to the milder flavour of green papaya, so you may have to adjust the acidity by adding more palm sugar.

SERVES 4
PREPARATION TIME 45 minutes, plus 15–20 minutes soaking time
COOKING TIME 5–10 minutes

30g/1oz dried shrimps
50g/1¾ oz/⅓ cup raw, skinless peanuts
400g/14oz firm green papaya or green mango
3 garlic cloves, chopped
2 red bird's eye chillies, deseeded and chopped
80g/2¾oz green beans or Chinese long beans, trimmed and cut into 4cm/1½in pieces
4 tbsp fish sauce
4 tbsp lime juice
2 tbsp grated palm sugar or soft light brown sugar
12 cherry tomatoes, halved

1 Put the dried shrimps in a small bowl, cover with water and leave to soak for 15–20 minutes.

2 Heat a frying pan over a medium-high heat, then add the peanuts and dry-roast until fragrant and starting to brown. Remove from the heat and leave to one side.

3 Peel the green papaya with a potato peeler, then either use a mandolin or zigzag peeler to shred the flesh, leaving behind the flesh nearest the seed. Put the shredded papaya in a bowl of cold salted water for 1–2 minutes to draw out the acidity and firm up the flesh. Drain, pat dry with kitchen paper and transfer to a bowl.

4 Squeeze out any excess water from the dried shrimps and pat dry with kitchen paper. Roughly chop into chunky pieces and put in a separate bowl.

5 Put the garlic and chillies in a large bowl and bruise with a pestle or the end of a rolling pin until they are almost mashed. Add the green beans, little by little, and bruise until all the beans start splitting. Add the prepared shrimps and peanuts and continue to pound and bruise until the shrimps and peanuts are roughly crushed and all the ingredients are well mixed.

6 Combine the fish sauce, lime juice and sugar in a small bowl until the sugar is dissolved. Slowly add the sauce to the shrimp and bean mixture, blending as you pour.

7 When everything is well pounded and mixed, slowly add the shredded papaya, mixing and lightly pounding between each addition. Finally, add the cherry tomatoes, toss well and serve immediately.

STICKY COCONUT RICE WITH caramelized mango

A popular, very sweet but also very tempting Thai dessert with a silky smooth texture and a great flavour. For a truly authentic dish, try to get Thai mangoes, nam dok mai, which are ripened on the tree so are much sweeter and tastier. Here I've given this dish an added dimension by caramelizing the mangoes.

SERVES 4
PREPARATION TIME 15 minutes, plus 1 hour 40 minutes soaking and resting time
COOKING TIME 35–40 minutes

300g/10½oz/1½ cups glutinous rice
350ml/12fl oz/scant 1½ cups coconut milk
4 tbsp granulated sugar
¼ tsp fine sea salt
2 ripe mangoes
60g/2¼oz/heaped ¼ cup caster sugar

1 Put the rice in a bowl, cover with cold water and soak for about 1 hour. Drain through a fine sieve and leave to stand for 15 minutes. Line a bamboo or electric steamer with muslin and spread the soaked rice over the muslin. Steam the rice for about 20 minutes, or until it becomes translucent and is soft all the way through. Turn off the heat and let the rice sit in the steamer for about a further 5 minutes.

2 Meanwhile, pour the coconut milk into a saucepan over a medium heat and slowly bring to the boil. Remove from the heat, add the sugar and salt and stir until the sugar is dissolved. Leave to one side.

3 Remove the rice in the muslin from the steamer and tip into a bowl. Pour 300ml/10½fl oz/scant 1¼ cups of the sugared coconut milk over the rice and mix well. Cover with cling film and leave to stand for about 25 minutes to allow the rice to absorb the coconut milk.

4 Meanwhile, peel the mangos with a potato peeler. Taking one mango, slice off the stem end to create a flat surface, then, holding the mango upright and using a sharp knife, slice downwards from top to bottom to cut off one side of the mango. As you slice down, use the flat edge of the seed as your guide. Slice off the other side, then repeat with the second mango. Cut the mango flesh into 1.5cm/⅝in strips lengthways.

5 Mix together the caster sugar and 55ml/1¾fl oz/scant ¼ cup water in a large saucepan over a medium-high heat, stirring until the sugar dissolves. Bring to a gentle boil, reduce the heat to medium and simmer, without stirring, for 3–4 minutes until the mixture thickens and turns light brown. Reduce the heat to medium-low, add the mangoes and cook for about 5 minutes.

6 Divide the sticky rice onto individual dessert plates. Top with the caramelized mango strips and pour over the remaining sugared coconut milk. Serve at room temperature.

CAMBODIA & VIETNAM

Fresh, sweet, sour and salty with a gentle spiciness; this sums up Cambodian cuisine, and the taste of each dish mirrors the country itself: warm, beautiful and full of character and flavour.

Cambodian food shares many similarities with that of its neighbours – Laos, Thailand and Vietnam. From a simple dish of Cambodian Beef Stir-Fry with Chilli Sauce (*see page 152*), with a superb balance of citrus, saltiness and sweetness to a flavoursome bowl of Khmer Yellow Chicken Curry (*see page 146*), which uses many of the essential ingredients of all these cuisines, including lemongrass, lime leaves, coriander, chillies, coconut milk, shrimp paste and galangal.

Rice noodles and rice are the two food staples in neighbouring Vietnam, where the food is typically light and refreshing – perfect for the hot and humid climate. Grilled Beef Salad (*see page 163*), which is made with a slight pungent-tasting fish sauce and a generous amount of the fresh and fragrant herbs basil and coriander, is a perfect example of this light and tasty cuisine. Vietnamese Chicken Noodle Soup (*see page 144*) is the national dish and uses the spices star anise, black pepper and cloves to give fragrance and subtle depth, something else that is common to many Vietnamese dishes.

vietnamese chicken noodle soup

During my recent trip to Vietnam, I went in search of a real pho (pronounced fuh) experience. This noodle soup, known as Pho Ga, is a truly satisfying and complete meal. Because it is simmered at a very low heat, with the surface barely moving, the stock is really clear with no cloudiness. The gentle simmering also means the spices slowly infuse the stock, producing a really rich and deep flavour.

SERVES 4–6
PREPARATION TIME 10 minutes
COOKING TIME 2 hours
  15 minutes

1 x 2kg/4lb 8oz whole chicken
1 tsp sea salt
½ tsp black peppercorns
2 star anise
3 cloves
2 whole onions and 1 onion, finely sliced
8cm/3¼in piece of root ginger, peeled and finely chopped
4 garlic cloves, unpeeled
3 tbsp fish sauce
1 tbsp granulated sugar
150g/5½oz/1¼ cups bean sprouts
250g/9oz cooked 3mm/⅛in or 5mm/¼in rice sticks (*see page 215*)

TO SERVE
10 sprigs Thai basil
1 small handful of tarragon leaves, roughly chopped
1 small handful of coriander leaves
2 red chillies, sliced
1 lime, cut into wedges

1 Rinse the chicken thoroughly inside and out under runing cold water. Lightly rub the salt on the skin, then rinse the chicken again and pat dry inside and out with kitchen paper. Put the chicken, breast-side down, in a large saucepan. Put the peppercorns, star anise and cloves in a spice bag or secure in a piece of muslin and add to the saucepan with the chicken.

2 In a frying pan over a medium-high heat, dry-fry the 2 whole onions, ginger and garlic until slightly charred all around, then put in the saucepan with the chicken.

3 Pour 3 litres/105fl oz/12 cups cold water over the chicken and bring to the boil. Reduce the heat to low and simmer, covered, for about 1 hour, skimming off any scum from the surface as required. After 25 minutes, using kitchen tongs, turn the chicken breast-side up and continue to cook until the end of the cooking time. When the tip of a sharp knife is inserted into the thickest part of the meat the juices should run clear.

4 Remove the chicken from the stock, rinse under running cold water and rest for 10 minutes, or until cool enough to handle. Cut the meat away from the legs and remove the breast meat from the bone in 2 whole pieces. Return the bones to the stock and continue to simmer, covered, for a further 1 hour. Shred or slice the meat, removing the skin and any small bones. Cover with cling film to keep moist and leave to one side.

5 Take the stock off the heat and remove and discard all the solid ingredients. Leave to cool and then strain over a large bowl through a sieve lined with muslin. Give the saucepan a rinse and pour the stock back in. Bring to a gentle boil over a medium-high heat, add the fish sauce and sugar, stirring until the sugar is dissolved, then reduce the heat to low and leave gently simmering.

6 Meanwhile, bring a saucepan of water to the boil and blanch the bean sprouts for about 20 seconds. Divide the warm, cooked rice sticks into deep soup bowls, then top with the blanched bean sprouts. Add the shredded chicken and sprinkle over the sliced onion.

7 Meanwhile, bring the stock to a vigorous boil and put the sprigs of Thai basil, tarragon, coriander, chillies and lime on a plate. Ladle the stock into the bowls and serve immediately with the accompaniments on the side.

KHMER YELLOW CHICKEN CURRY

Spice pastes, kroeung, are very important in Khmer cooking, and are regularly used in stir-fries, soups and stews. There are three distinct types of spice pastes – yellow, green and red – and it is the dominant spice used to make the paste that defines its colour. In yellow kroeung it is turmeric; green chilli gives green kroeung its colour; and red chillies produce the bright red colour of red kroeung.

SERVES 4
PREPARATION TIME 30 minutes
COOKING TIME 30–40 minutes

2 tbsp sunflower oil
1 small onion, roughly
   chopped
1 recipe quantity Khmer
   Yellow Curry Spice Paste
   (*see page 208*)
600g/1lb 5oz boneless,
   skinless chicken thighs, cut
   into bite-sized pieces
2 kaffir lime leaves
1 carrot, cut into bite-sized
   pieces
400ml/14fl oz/generous
   1½ cups coconut milk
2 tbsp fish sauce
1 tbsp grated palm sugar or
   soft light brown sugar
150g/5½oz green beans, cut
   lengthways into 5cm/2in
   pieces

TO SERVE
1 recipe quantity Boiled
   Long-Grain Rice
   (*see page 214*)

1 Heat the oil in a large frying pan over a medium-high heat. Add the onion and cook for 2–3 minutes until soft and translucent, stirring occasionally. Add the spice paste and cook gently, stirring occasionally, for 10–15 minutes until fragrant and the oil starts to rise to the surface.

2 Tip in the chicken pieces and add the kaffir lime leaves, then push the chicken pieces around the pan until they are well coated with the spice paste. Cook for a further 4–5 minutes, then add the carrots and cook for another 2–3 minutes.

3 Pour the coconut milk into the pan and bring to the boil, then add the fish sauce and sugar and stir until the sugar is dissolved. Tip in the green beans and combine with the other ingredients. Reduce the heat to low and simmer for 10–15 minutes until the sauce starts to thicken and the chicken is cooked through. Serve immediately with boiled rice.

vietnamese-style chicken & pork pâté baguette

MAKES 4
PREPARATION TIME 1 hour, plus 2 hours 15 minutes marinating and pickling time and 24–36 hours resting time
COOKING TIME 45 minutes– 1 hour

4 sandwich-sized baguettes
1 small cucumber, quartered lengthways, deseeded and cut into matchsticks
chilli sauce, to taste (optional)
2 small handfuls of coriander leaves

PÂTÉ
250g/9oz chicken livers
30g/1oz butter
3 shallots, roughly chopped
3 garlic cloves, roughly chopped
1cm/½in piece of root ginger, peeled and roughly chopped
250g/9oz pork loin, cubed
1 tsp five-spice powder
4½ tsp fish sauce
¼ tsp sea salt
1 egg, beaten
2 bay leaves

PICKLED CARROT & DAIKON
200g/7oz carrots, grated
200g/7oz daikon, grated
½ tbsp sea salt
3 tbsp clear honey
125ml/4fl oz/½ cup rice vinegar

1 To make the pâté, cut the chicken livers in half and trim off any fibrous tissues. Rinse under running cold water and pat dry with kitchen paper.

2 Melt the butter in a frying pan over a medium heat, then add the shallots, garlic and ginger. Cook for 2 minutes, or until fragrant and softened, then transfer to a food processor. Add the pork loin and chicken livers and blend to a rough paste.

3 Transfer the paste to a bowl, add the five-spice powder, fish sauce, salt and egg and stir until well combined. Cover with cling film and leave to marinate in the fridge for about 2 hours.

4 To prepare the pickled vegetables, put the shredded carrots and daikon in a bowl, rub in the salt and leave to stand for 5 minutes. Squeeze out as much moisture as possible, then pat dry with kitchen paper. Return the vegetables to the bowl, mix in the honey and pour in the rice vinegar. Leave to stand at room temperature for at least 1 hour.

5 Remove the marinated pork and chicken liver pâté from the fridge and spoon the mixture into an 18 x 14cm/7 x 5½in baking dish. Level the surface and arrange the bay leaves on top. Leave to stand at room temperature for 15 minutes. Meanwhile, preheat the oven to 180°C/350°F/Gas 4.

6 Cover the baking dish tightly with kitchen foil and transfer to a large roasting tin. Pour in enough boiling water to come two-thirds of the way up the baking dish, place the roasting tin in the preheated oven and bake for 45 minutes–1 hour, or until the tip of a sharp, fine-bladed knife inserted into the centre of the pâté comes out clean.

7 Remove the kitchen foil and bay leaves from the pâté. Leave to cool at room temperature, then cover with cling film and refrigerate for 24–36 hours. When ready to serve, turn the pâté out onto a chopping board and cut into 1cm/½in slices.

8 Slice each baguette in half lengthways, leaving one side still intact. Spread 2 generous slices of pâté over each baguette, then top with the cucumber strips and pickled carrot and daikon. Spoon over the chilli sauce, if using, and sprinkle over the coriander and serve. Any unused pickled vegetables can be stored in a jar in the fridge for up to 1 month.

PHNOM PENH NOODLE SOUP

SERVES 4–6
PREPARATION TIME 20 minutes, plus making the stock and soaking and cooking the noodles
COOKING TIME about 1 hour, plus cooking the noodles

1 recipe quantity Pork Stock (*see page 211*)
1 onion
½ tsp coriander seeds
2 cloves
¼ tsp Sichuan peppercorns
250g/9oz pork mince
1 spring onion, finely chopped
1 tbsp sunflower oil
200g/7oz raw, peeled king prawns, deveined (*see page 216*)
150g/5½oz/1¼ cups bean sprouts
250g/9oz cooked thick rice noodles (*see page 215*)
2 tbsp fish sauce
2 tsp sugar
sea salt and freshly ground black pepper
1 small handful of coriander leaves, to serve
2 tbsp Fried Shallots (*see page 212*), to serve

TO SERVE
1 lime, cut into wedges
bean sprouts

1 Pour the pork stock into a saucepan and bring to the boil over a high heat. Reduce the heat to low and simmer. Meanwhile, dry-fry the whole onion in a frying pan over a medium-high heat until the outer layer is slightly charred all round. Add the charred onion to the simmering stock. Put the coriander seeds, cloves and Sichuan peppercorns in a spice bag or secure in a piece of muslin and add into the stock. Continue to simmer, covered, for 45 minutes.

2 Put the pork mince in a bowl and season with salt and pepper. Tip into a food processor and blend to a smooth paste. Put the pork back into the bowl, add the spring onion and mix until well combined. Using a teaspoon or melon baller, scoop up the paste and shape into chestnut-sized balls and arrange on a plate – they don't need to be perfectly round. Repeat until all the pork paste is used. Cover with cling film and leave to one side.

3 Heat the oil in a large frying pan over a medium-high heat. Add the prawns and stir-fry for 3–4 minutes until they turn pink and are cooked through. Transfer to a plate and leave to one side.

4 Bring a saucepan of water to the boil and blanch the bean sprouts for about 20 seconds. Divide the warm, cooked noodles into deep soup bowls, then top with the blanched bean sprouts.

5 Bring the stock back to the boil, then add the pork balls and cook for 4–5 minutes until they are cooked through and float to the surface. Divide the pork balls into the bowls of noodles and add the cooked prawns.

6 Add the fish sauce, a generous pinch of salt and the sugar to the pork stock and bring to a vigorous boil. Ladle the stock into the bowls, then sprinkle over the coriander and fried shallots. Serve immediately with the lime wedges and extra bean sprouts on the side.

cambodian beef stir-fry with chilli sauce

This dish was brought to Cambodia from Vietnam during the French colonization. The name in Vietnamese, Bo Luc Lac, literally means 'shaking beef', and this recipe is based on a delicious version I ate in Phnom Penh. I've added honey and used dark soy sauce, which make it stand out in flavour.

SERVES 4
PREPARATION TIME 30 minutes, plus minimum 1 hour marinating time
COOKING TIME about 10 minutes

500g/1lb 2oz sirloin, cut into bite-sized pieces
5 garlic cloves, finely chopped
½ tsp sea salt
¼ tsp freshly ground black pepper
¼ tsp cinnamon
2 tsp dark soy sauce
2 tbsp sunflower oil
150g/5½oz lettuce leaves, roughly torn
2 tomatoes, sliced
1 small cucumber, deseeded and cut into chunks
1 small red onion, thinly sliced
1 tbsp fish sauce
1 tbsp tomato ketchup
2 tsp honey

CHILLI SAUCE
½ tsp sea salt
¼ tsp freshly ground black pepper
1 small red chilli, deseeded and sliced
juice of 1 lime

TO SERVE
1 recipe quantity Boiled Long-Grain Rice (*see page 214* – optional)

1 To prepare the chilli sauce, mix all the ingredients in a small bowl and leave to one side.
2 Put the sirloin, garlic, salt, black pepper, cinnamon and soy sauce in a large bowl and mix well. Cover with cling film and leave to marinate in the fridge for 1 hour or, for and even better flavour, overnight.
3 Heat the oil in a wok or large frying pan over a high heat until smoking hot. Tip in the beef and marinade and stir-fry for 5–7 minutes until the beef is browned and the liquid has evaporated. Add the fish sauce, tomato ketchup and honey to the wok and push the beef around until well coated. Cook for a further 1 minute, then spoon the beef over the salad, drizzle over the chilli sauce and serve immediately with boiled rice, if you like.

caramelized salmon with pineapple

The combination of sweetness and saltiness with a touch of chilli in this dish goes well with just about any fish, but it is particularly good with the buttery richness of salmon. If you want to try it with a white-fleshed fish, I suggest either haddock or monkfish. Fish steaks work better than fillets, which easily break into pieces.

SERVES 4
PREPARATION TIME 45 minutes
COOKING TIME about 25 minutes

4 x 250g/9oz boneless, unskinned salmon steaks (about 2.5–3cm/1–1¼in thick)
1 tbsp sunflower oil
3 garlic cloves, finely chopped
1 small red chilli, deseeded and finely diced
2 tbsp granulated sugar
1 tbsp clear honey
¼ tsp freshly ground black pepper
4 tbsp fish sauce
2 tsp dark soy sauce
200g/7oz pineapple, peeled, cored and cut into bite-sized pieces

TO SERVE
1 recipe quantity Boiled Long-Grain Rice (*see page 214* – optional)

1 For each salmon steak, using the tip of a small, sharp knife, carefully slice the skin away from the flesh from the bottom two sides of the steaks, leaving it intact on the upper halves. Fold the skinned pieces of fish into the centre of the steak to create a circular shape, then wrap the loose pieces of skin around the outside. Secure in place with kitchen string. This is known as a fish noisette.

2 Heat the oil in a frying pan over a medium-high heat. Add the garlic and chilli and stir-fry for 1–2 minutes until fragrant. Add the sugar, honey, pepper, fish sauce and soy sauce and stir until the sugar is dissolved. Simmer, stirring constantly, for 2 minutes, or until the sauce starts to caramelize.

3 Add the prepared salmon steaks and pineapple to the pan and bring to the boil. Reduce the heat to medium and cook, covered, for 10–12 minutes until the salmon turns opaque and is cooked through.

4 Remove the lid and carefully push the salmon and pineapple around the pan until well coated with the sauce. Remove the string from the steaks and serve immediately with the pineapple and sauce spooned over with boiled rice, if you like.

cha cha la vong

SERVES 4
PREPARATION TIME 25 minutes,
plus 30 minutes marinating time
COOKING TIME 15–20 minutes

3cm/1¼in piece of fresh
  turmeric, peeled and roughly
  chopped, or 2 tsp ground
  turmeric
1cm/½in piece of galangal,
  peeled and roughly chopped
1cm/½in piece of root ginger,
  peeled and roughly chopped
2 garlic cloves, roughly
  chopped
2 tbsp fish sauce
2 tsp sugar
a generous pinch of ground
  pepper
550g/1lb 4oz skinned
  monkfish, cod or pollack
  fillets, cut into bite-sized
  pieces
185g/6½oz dried rice
  vermicelli
3 tbsp sunflower oil
40g/1½oz dill, trimmed
10 spring onions, cut into
  6cm/2½in lengths and sliced
15g/½oz chives, cut into
  5cm/2in lengths (optional)

TO SERVE
50g/1¾oz skinless raw
  peanuts
1 small handful of Thai basil
  leaves
1 small handful of coriander
  leaves
2 red chillies, deseeded and
  sliced (optional)
1 recipe quantity Nuoc Cham
  Dipping Sauce (*see page 213*)

1 Put the fresh turmeric, if using, galangal, ginger and garlic in a mortar or a food processor and pound with a pestle or blend into a smooth paste. Transfer to a large bowl, add the ground turmeric, if using, and combine with the fish sauce, sugar and ground pepper. Tip the fish into the bowl and toss until each piece of fish is well coated in the paste. Cover with cling film and leave to marinate at room temperature for about 30 minutes.

2 Heat a frying pan over a medium-high heat, then add the peanuts and dry-roast until fragrant and starting to brown. Remove from the heat, roughly chop and leave to one side.

3 Bring a saucepan of water to the boil and cook the rice vermicelli for 2–3 minutes until softened. Drain, refresh under running cold water, pat dry with kitchen paper and divide into four individual serving bowls.

4 Heat the oil in a frying pan over a medium-high heat. Add the marinated fish and fry, stirring occasionally, for 6–7 minutes until crisp, golden brown and cooked through. Add the dill, spring onions and chives, if using. Toss and cook for a few more seconds until wilted. Remove from the heat and transfer to a serving dish.

5 Transfer the bowls of noodles, accompaniments and turmeric fish to the table for everyone to assemble their own dish.

curry FISH mousse

Traditionally, this Cambodian dish is served in banana leaves that are folded into a tray shape. Two leaves, cut into squares, are layered and then folded up at the edges to create corners, which are secured with cocktail sticks. A simpler way to serve Amok Trey is in small, heatproof bowls.

SERVES 6
PREPARATION TIME 10 minutes
COOKING TIME 20 minutes

350ml/12fl oz/scant 1½ cups
  coconut milk
1 tbsp grated palm sugar or
  soft light brown sugar
1 tbsp fish sauce
1 recipe quantity Curry Fish
  Mousse Spice Paste (*see
  page 207*)
2 eggs, beaten
2 kaffir lime leaves, thinly
  sliced
450g/1lb boneless, skinless
  haddock loin, or other white
  fish fillets, cut into bite-sized
  pieces
sea salt

TO SERVE
Tomato & Glass Noodle Salad
  (*see page 170*)

1 Put the coconut milk and sugar in a large bowl and stir until the sugar is dissolved. Add the fish sauce, spice paste, eggs, kaffir lime leaves and a pinch of salt and stir until combined. Tip in the fish and toss until the fish is well coated with the paste mixture.

2 Make up six banana leaf bowls (see introduction above), if you like, then fill with the coated fish – the sauce should nearly cover all the fish pieces. Alternatively, use six individual 150ml/5fl oz/scant ⅔ cup ramekins or heatproof bowls.

3 Place the ramekins in a bamboo or electric steamer and steam for 20 minutes, or until the mixture is set and the fish is cooked through. It should be slightly firm to the touch. Leave to stand for 5 minutes at room temperature before serving with the Tomato & Glass Noodle Salad.

HOT & SPICY VEGETABLE STEW

This Cambodian dish is one of the simplest and tastiest clear broth stews that I have ever eaten. It is a little like the Thai version Tom Yum. The combination of the spiciness from the chilli with the meatiness of the mushrooms and baby corn makes it filling and satisfying.

SERVES 4
PREPARATION TIME 30 minutes, plus making the pork stock, if using
COOKING TIME about 1 hour

1 litre/35fl oz/4 cups vegetable stock or ½ recipe quantity Pork Stock (*see page 211*)
1 onion
2 star anise
¼ tsp black peppercorns
1 tbsp sunflower oil
2–2½ tsp chilli flakes, to taste
1 garlic clove, finely chopped
100g/3½oz baby corn, sliced in half lengthways
4 tomatoes, cut into wedges
100g/3½oz dried mushrooms, such as shiitake, porcini or Chinese mushrooms, soaked, drained and cut into thin strips (*see page 217*)
55g/2oz mangetout
1 tbsp fish sauce
½ tsp sea salt
2 tbsp lime juice
1 tbsp grated palm sugar or soft light brown sugar
1 handful of coriander leaves, to serve

TO SERVE
350g/12oz cooked rice noodles (*see page 215*)

1 Pour the stock into a saucepan and bring to the boil over a high heat. Reduce the heat to low and simmer. Meanwhile, dry-fry the whole onion in a frying pan over a medium-high heat until the outer layer is slightly charred all round, then add the charred onion to the simmering stock. Put the star anise and peppercorns in a spice bag or secure in a piece of muslin and add to the stock.

2 Heat the oil in a frying pan over a medium-high heat. Add the chilli flakes and garlic and stir-fry for 1–2 minutes until fragrant, then add to the stock. Continue to simmer the stock for 40 minutes. Discard the onion and the spice bag.

3 Just before serving, bring the stock to a gentle boil. Add the baby corn and tomatoes and cook for 2–3 minutes until they start to soften. Add the mushrooms and mangetout and cook for a further 2–3 minutes, or until all the vegetables are softened. Add the fish sauce, salt, lime juice and sugar and stir until the sugar is dissolved.

4 Bring the stew to a vigorous boil for a few seconds, then serve immediately with the rice noodles and coriander sprinkled over.

grilled beef salad

I was treated to the best grilled beef salad I have ever eaten in Hanoi, Vietnam. The sweet, sour and salty dressing really complements the slightly charred beef slices, and the use of star fruit adds a delicious and unusual edge. If you can't get star fruit, substitute it with green apple. I've added pomegranate seeds and used coriander and mint, instead of the traditional Thai basil, to give this salad a refreshing twist.

SERVES 4
PREPARATION TIME 30 minutes, plus 1 hour 25 minutes freezing and marinating time
COOKING TIME about 10 minutes

4 garlic cloves, roughly chopped
3 shallots, roughly chopped
1cm/½in piece of root ginger, peeled and roughly chopped
1 red chilli, deseeded and roughly chopped
500g/1lb 2oz rib-eye steak or sirloin, wrapped and semi-frozen for 25 minutes (*see page 217*)
1 tbsp light soy sauce
½ tbsp grated palm sugar or soft light brown sugar
1 tbsp sunflower oil
1 star fruit
100g/3½oz/heaped ½ cup pomegranate seeds
1 small handful of coriander leaves
1 tbsp mint leaves
2 tbsp Fried Shallots (*see page 212*), to serve

DRESSING
4 tbsp fish sauce
2 tbsp sugar
3 tbsp lime juice

1 Put the garlic, shallots, ginger and chilli in a mortar and pestle or a food processor and blend to a smooth paste. Transfer to a large bowl.

2 Remove the partially frozen beef from the freezer and unwrap the cling film. Using a sharp knife, cut the beef against the grain into 3mm/⅛in slices. Put the beef in the bowl with the ground paste, then add the soy sauce and sugar and mix until well combined. Cover with cling film and leave to marinate in the fridge for 1 hour.

3 Meanwhile, to prepare the dressing, mix all the ingredients with 4 tablespoons water and leave to one side.

4 Heat the oil in a ridged griddle pan or heavy-based frying pan over a high heat. When the oil is smoking hot, add the marinated beef and cook for a few seconds before turning the heat down to medium-high. Spread out the meat in the pan, laying it as flat as possible so it cooks evenly. Cook for 7–10 minutes, turning occasionally, until the beef is browned and tender.

5 Cut the star fruit into 5mm/¼in slices and put in a salad bowl. Add the pomegranate seeds, coriander, mint, stir-fried beef and dressing and toss well. Serve with the fried shallots sprinkled over.

STEAMED RICE CAKES WITH PRAWNS

There are many amazing local specialities in Hue, Vietnam, and I made sure I ate as many as I could during my visit. These steamed rice cakes, Banh Beo, were my favourite, and are great eaten as an afternoon snack.

MAKES 16
PREPARATION TIME 30 minutes, plus cooling time
COOKING TIME about 30 minutes

150g/5½oz/heaped ¾ cup rice flour
5 tsp cornflour
¼ tsp sea salt
3 tbsp sunflower oil, plus extra for oiling
200g/7oz raw, peeled large king prawns, deveined (*see page 216*)
2 garlic cloves, finely chopped
2 shallots, finely diced
10g/¼oz pork rind, crushed
1 red chilli, deseeded and finely sliced

SAUCE
1 tbsp fish sauce
2 tbsp clear honey
1 red chilli, deseeded and sliced

1 Put the rice flour, cornflour, salt and 1 tablespoon of the oil in a bowl. Gradually pour in 350ml/12fl oz/scant 1½ cups water and mix well. Leave to one side.

2 To make the sauce, put all the ingredients in a small bowl with 4 tablespoons water and gently whisk until combined. Leave to one side.

3 Bring a saucepan of water to the boil. Add the prawns and cook for 3–4 minutes until they turn pink and are cooked through. Drain, dry with kitchen paper and leave to cool. When cool, put the prawns in a food processor and blend briefly – you still want some chunky bits.

4 Heat the remaining 2 tablespoons of oil in a frying pan over a medium-high heat. Tip in the chopped prawns and stir-fry for 1 minute. Add the garlic and shallots and stir-fry for 4–5 minutes until fragrant. Remove from the heat, cover and leave to one side.

5 Lightly oil 16 individual shallow dishes, such as dipping sauce dishes, either all the same size or a range of sizes, if you like. Stir the rice flour mixture until smooth, then divide into the dishes. Arrange as many dishes as will fit in a bamboo or electric steamer and steam for 8–10 minutes until set. Leave to cool, and repeat until all the rice cakes are cooked.

6 Serve the rice cakes either in the dishes or gently scoop them out, using a spoon, onto a serving plate. Put about 1 tablespoon of the cooked prawn mixture on top of each rice cake and then sprinkle over the ground pork rind and chilli. Just before serving, drizzle 1–2 teaspoons of the sauce over each rice cake.

grilled prawn lemongrass skewers

In Vietnam these grilled prawn skewers are usually served on their own. For a more complete and moreish dish, here I wrap the extra-crispy skewers in lettuce leaves with herbs and bean sprouts. Another way to make this dish is to wrap the prawn paste in dry rice paper. Because the rice paper isn't soaked, you get to enjoy the different textures of the ingredients – the crispiness of the rice paper, which is slightly softened by the Nuoc Cham Dipping Sauce, and the tender, moist prawns.

MAKES 16
PREPARATION TIME 30 minutes, plus 1 hour marinating time
COOKING TIME 30 minutes

500g/1lb 2oz raw, peeled large king prawns, deveined and roughly chopped (*see page 216*)
2 garlic cloves, finely chopped
1 tbsp fish sauce
1 tsp grated palm sugar or soft light brown sugar
1 spring onion, chopped
1 tbsp sunflower oil, plus extra for oiling
16 lemongrass stalks, outer leaves and stalk ends removed, trimmed to 4.5cm/1¾in lengths
sea salt

TO SERVE
80g/2¾oz dried rice vermicelli (*see page 215*)
1 small round lettuce
6 sprigs Thai basil
1 small handful of pea shoots
55g/2oz/heaped ¼ cup bean sprouts
1 recipe quantity Nuoc Cham Dipping Sauce (*see page 213*)

1 Put the prawns, garlic, fish sauce, sugar and spring onion in a food processor and blend to a rough paste without any solid pieces of prawns. Transfer to a bowl and stir in the oil. Cover with cling film and leave to marinate in the fridge for 1 hour.

2 Bring a saucepan of water to the boil and cook the vermicelli for 2–3 minutes until softened. Drain, refresh under running cold water, pat dry with kitchen paper and transfer to a serving plate.

3 Prepare a bowl of slightly salted water. Moisten one hand with the salted water to avoid the prawn paste sticking and then place 2 heaped tablespoons of the prawn paste in the palm. Use the back of the spoon to flatten the paste into a 5cm/2in circle, then slightly close your hand and place three-quarters of a lemongrass stalk along the centre. Mould the paste around the lemongrass. Set aside and repeat until all the ingredients are used.

4 Line a bamboo or electric steamer with a piece of greaseproof paper and arrange the prawn skewers on the paper. Steam the skewers for about 5 minutes, or until the prawn paste is almost cooked through. Remove from the heat and leave to stand at room temperature for 5 minutes.

5 Pour some oil into a ridged griddle pan or heavy-based frying pan over a medium-high heat, then use kitchen paper to grease the pan evenly and soak up any excess oil. Griddle the prawn skewers in batches of 5–6 sticks, turning frequently, for 6–7 minutes until browned all round and cooked through. Remove from the pan and keep warm until all the skewers are cooked. Oil the pan again, as required.

6 Transfer the skewers, plate of accompaniments and Nuoc Cham Dipping Sauce to the table for everyone to make up into parcels and then dip in the sauce. To assemble the parcels, cut the prawn meat off the lemongrass and into smaller pieces and then fold up in a lettuce leaf with the herbs, bean sprouts and rice vermicelli.

vietnamese prawn rice paper rolls

These spring rolls, neatly wrapped in translucent rice paper, look stunning with a hint of orange and green colours from the ingredients inside showing through. Each bite of these healthy finger foods, reveals a mouth-watering combination of the fresh, clean flavours of the rice paper rolls against the gentle tang of the Nuoc Cham Dipping Sauce.

MAKES 12
PREPARATION TIME 45 minutes
COOKING TIME 3 minutes

120g/4¼oz dried rice
 vermicelli
12 x 16cm/6¼in round rice
 paper sheets
36 Thai basil leaves or mint
 leaves
24 cooked, peeled large king
 prawns
20g/¾oz/scant ¼ cup bean
 sprouts
12 garlic chives, cut into
 16cm/6¼in lengths

TO SERVE
1 recipe quantity Nuoc Cham
 Dipping Sauce (*see page 213*)

1 Bring a saucepan of water to the boil and cook the rice vermicelli for 2–3 minutes until softened. Drain, refresh under running cold water and pat dry with kitchen paper. Transfer to a bowl and roughly cut into 6cm/2½in pieces.

2 Lay a damp, clean tea towel on a chopping board and place a large bowl of warm water to the side. Take a sheet of rice paper and submerge in the warm water for about 10 seconds. Don't soak the rice paper for too long, as it will tear.

3 Lay a soaked rice paper sheet flat on a the tea towel. Arrange 3 basil leaves along the centre of the sheet, then place 2 prawns roughly on top of the basil leaves. Next put a few bean sprouts on the prawns and then a large pinch of cooked rice vermicelli. Mould the ingredients into an oblong shape. Fold the bottom of the sheet over the filling, then fold in the two sides. Add 2 garlic chives to the centre, crossways, so one end of each of the chives sticks over the edge. Roll the spring roll and chives up as tightly as possible. Put the spring roll on a serving plate and cover with a damp tea towel, then repeat until all the ingredients are used. Serve at room temperature with Nuoc Cham Dipping Sauce on the side.

tomato & glass noodle salad

For a salad that is so easy to make, you will be surprised by just how satisfying and enjoyable it is to eat. The dressing is made up of punchy flavours, including unripened tomatoes, which are slightly more acidic than ripe ones and are often used in Cambodian cooking. If you can't get unripened tomatoes, cherry tomatoes are a good substitute.

SERVES 4
PREPARATION TIME 30 minutes
COOKING TIME 5–10 minutes

150g/5½oz glass noodles, such as bean thread vermicelli
55g/2oz/⅓ cup raw cashew nuts
a generous pinch of chilli powder
2 tsp honey
300g/10½oz unripened tomatoes, roughly chopped, or cherry tomatoes, halved
½ red onion, finely sliced
85g/3oz/scant ½ cup bean sprouts
1 handful of coriander leaves
1 handful of Thai basil leaves or sweet basil leaves

DRESSING
1 garlic clove, finely chopped
2 red bird's eye chillies, deseeded and sliced
4 tbsp lime juice
½ tsp lime zest
4 tbsp fish sauce
2 tbsp clear honey

1 To make the dressing, put all the ingredients in a small bowl and gently whisk until combined. Leave to one side.

2 Bring a saucepan of water to the boil and cook the glass noodles for 2–3 minutes until softened. Drain, refresh under running cold water, pat dry with kitchen paper and tip into a large bowl.

3 Heat a frying pan over a medium-high heat, then add the cashew nuts and dry-roast until fragrant and starting to brown. Remove from heat, add the chilli powder and honey to the pan and stir until the cashews are well coated. Leave to cool. When the nuts are cold enough to handle, roughly chop.

4 Add the tomatoes, onion, bean sprouts, coriander and Thai basil or sweet basil to the bowl with the prepared noodles. Pour over the dressing and toss all the ingredients together until well combined. Serve with the chopped spicy peanuts sprinkled over.

vietnamese sago pudding

SERVES 4
PREPARATION TIME 20 minutes,
plus dried bean soaking and
cooling time
COOKING TIME 45 minutes

250g/9oz/heaped 1 cup caster
  sugar
85g/3oz/1⅔ cups medium
  sago pearls
1 tsp green tea powder
100g/3½oz/scant ½ cup
  peeled split mung beans,
  soaked for at least 4 hours or
  overnight
55g/2oz/¼ cup kidney beans,
  soaked for 2 hours, or
  80g/2¾oz/heaped ⅓ cup
  drained tinned kidney beans
150ml/5fl oz/scant ⅔ cup
  coconut milk
¼ tsp fine sea salt
crushed ice, to serve

1 Put 200g/7oz/heaped ¾ cup of the sugar and 80ml/2½fl oz/
⅓ cup water in a saucepan over a medium-high heat. Bring to the
boil, stirring constantly to dissolve the sugar, then reduce the heat
to medium-low and gently boil for 6–7 minutes until the mixture
starts to thicken but not colour. Remove from the heat and leave
to one side.

2 Bring a large saucepan of water to the boil. Add the sago pearls,
reduce the heat to medium-low and cook for 30 minutes,
uncovered, or until they become translucent, stirring occasionally
to stop the pearls from sticking. Add more boiling water if the sago
gets too sticky. Drain in a colander and rinse under running cold
water, lightly rubbing the sago to wash away the starch. Transfer to
a bowl, sprinkle over the green tea powder and mix until well
combined. Leave to cool.

3 Meanwhile, cook the soaked and drained split mung beans and
kidney beans, if using. Put the split mung beans in a saucepan, add
150ml/5fl oz/scant ⅔ cup water and bring to the boil over a high
heat. Cover the pan, reduce the heat to medium and cook, stirring
occasionally, for 30 minutes or until the mung beans are soft and
almost falling apart. Add more water to the pan if the beans become
too dry. Remove from the heat, add the remaining sugar and stir
until well combined. Using a fork or potato masher, mash the beans
to a fine paste and leave to cool.

4 At the same time, bring a further saucepan of water to the boil over
a high heat and add the soaked and drained kidney beans. Cover the
pan, reduce the heat to medium and cook for 15–20 minutes until
tender. Remove from the heat, drain and leave to cool. If using
tinned kidney beans drain and rinse well.

5 While the beans are cooking, put the coconut milk in a saucepan
and gently heat over a medium-low heat, stirring occasionally.
When bubbles start to form on the surface, remove from the heat
and leave to cool.

6 Divide the syrup into 4 glasses. Add the mung beans, then the
coloured sago followed by the kidney beans. Top each glass with
the coconut milk, then add a large handful of crushed ice to each
glass just before serving. Give everything a good stir before eating.

INDIA &
SRI LANKA

India is a vast country where the food varies greatly regionally. In the northern regions, the food is generally creamy, rich and flavoursome but mildly spicy, as in Lamb Rogan Josh (*see page 186*), whereas in the southern parts dishes are often significantly more spicy and are mostly coconut based, as in Fish Curry with Okra (*see page 192*) and Kerala Beef (*see page 184*). But no matter which part of India you are in, dried spices of many varieties come into play. Before the cooking starts, there is the grinding and toasting of the spices, and this step makes a real difference to the taste of the final dish.

Similarly in Sri Lanka, the use of dried spices, such as cardamom, cinnamon, cloves, cumin, ground fennel, pepper and turmeric is key, but in comparison to India, there are fewer fresh spices used, mainly just chilli and curry leaves. However, despite this, there is a beautiful, subtle boldness and balance to Sri Lankan cuisine, and Sour Fish Curry (*see page 191*) is an amazing example. Pandan leaves, which grow luxuriantly in most backyards in Sri Lanka, are one of the most important items when cooking traditional Sri Lankan curries, such as Devilled Pork (*see page 182*), and provide a unique, flowery fragrance and flavour. A delicious modern twist to these dishes is to use lemongrass instead.

chicken biryani rice

Biryani, a meal in itself, originates from Persia and is a highly celebrated dish in India. Don't be put off by the long list of spices. The time and effort you put into preparing this dish will definitely be repaid in the eating.

SERVES 4
PREPARATION TIME 30 minutes, plus about 1 hour marinating, soaking and resting time
COOKING TIME about 1 hour

600g/1lb 5oz boneless, skinless chicken thighs, cut into bite-sized pieces
½ tsp turmeric
¼ tsp chilli powder
2 garlic cloves, grated
2 tbsp Greek yogurt
1 tsp sea salt
350g/12oz/1¾ cups basmati rice
¼ tsp cumin seeds
2 x 5cm/2in cinnamon sticks
6 green cardamom pods
2 tbsp sunflower oil
2 black cardamom pods
4 cloves
3–4 dried bay leaves
1 star anise
6–7 black peppercorns
2 onions, sliced
2 green chillies, deseeded and chopped
1 tomato, chopped
½ tsp tomato purée
a pinch of saffron threads
1 tbsp butter, softened
1 handful of coriander leaves, roughly chopped, to serve
1–2 tbsp desiccated coconut, to serve
2 tbsp Fried Shallots (*see page 212*), to serve

1 Put the chicken pieces in a large bowl, then add the turmeric, chilli powder, garlic, yogurt and ½ teaspoon of the salt and toss until each piece of chicken is well coated with the marinade. Cover with cling film and leave to marinate in the fridge for 45 minutes–1 hour. Remove from the fridge and leave to stand at room temperature for 15 minutes before cooking.

2 Meanwhile, put the rice in a large saucepan and pour in enough water to half fill the pan. Swirl the rice using your hand, lightly rubbing the grains, until the water becomes cloudy. Tilt the pot carefully to pour off the water. Repeat this process for 3–4 times. The water will not be completely clear, but will be less cloudy than the first wash. Cover the rice with water and leave to stand for 30 minutes. Drain and leave to sit in the sieve for 5 minutes.

3 Half fill a saucepan with water and bring to the boil over a medium-high heat. Add the washed rice, cumin seeds, 1 cinnamon stick, 3 green cardamom pods and the remaining ½ teaspoon of salt and boil gently for 3–4 minutes. Drain the rice into a sieve and rinse under running cold water to stop the cooking process. Discard the cinnamon stick and cardamom pods and leave to one side.

4 Heat the oil in a large, heavy-based frying pan over a medium heat. Add the remaining cinnamon stick and 3 green cardamom pods, the black cardamom pods, cloves, bay leaves, star anise and peppercorns and sizzle for a few seconds until fragrant. Add the onions and stir-fry for 3–4 minutes until soft and translucent. Tip in the chillies, tomato and tomato purée and stir-fry for 1–2 minutes.

5 Tip in the chicken and push around the pan until well coated with the spices. Cook for 10–15 minutes until the chicken is sealed and golden brown, stirring occasionally. Meanwhile, put the saffron threads in a bowl with 2 tablespoons hot water and leave to one side.

6 When the chicken is cooked, remove the pan from the heat and transfer the chicken and all the pan ingredients to a plate. Using the same pan, spread half of the partially cooked rice evenly over the base. Drizzle 1 tablespoon of the saffron liquid over the rice, then arrange half of the chicken pieces on top of the rice. Spread the remaining rice evenly over the chicken, drizzle over the remaining saffron liquid and add the remaining chicken. Sprinkle about 30ml/1fl oz/2 tablespoons water into the pan and scatter over the butter.

7 Place the pan over a low heat, cover and cook for 30 minutes, or until the rice is cooked and the chicken tender. About 15 minutes into the cooking time, give the rice and chicken a quick and thorough stir. Serve hot with the coriander, desiccated coconut and fried shallots sprinkled over.

coorg-style chicken curry

Coorg is situated in South West India, and the cuisine in this area of India is very much influenced by its geography, culture and people. In general, curries are slightly spicier and coconut milk is used more often than in curries from other parts of India.

SERVES 4
PREPARATION TIME 25 minutes, plus 30 minutes marinating time
COOKING TIME about 45 minutes

500g/1lb 2oz boneless, skinless chicken breasts or chicken thighs, trimmed and cut into bite-sized pieces
½ tsp turmeric
½ tsp chilli powder
2 tbsp sunflower oil
½ tsp black mustard seeds
1 red onion, chopped
2 garlic cloves, finely chopped
3cm/1¼in piece of root ginger, peeled and grated
1 recipe quantity Coorg-style Curry Spice Paste (*see page 207*)
3 tomatoes, skinned, halved, deseeded and roughly chopped (*see page 217*)
2 tbsp lime juice
100ml/3½fl oz/generous ⅓ cup coconut milk
sea salt
1 small handful of coriander leaves, to serve

TO SERVE
1 recipe quantity Boiled Long-Grain Rice (*see page 214*)
Garlic Naan (*see page 180*)

1 Put the chicken in a large bowl, then add the turmeric, chilli powder and a pinch of salt and toss until each of the chicken pieces is well coated with the spices. Cover with cling film and leave to marinate for 30 minutes at room temperature.

2 Heat the oil in a frying pan over a medium-high heat. Add the mustard seeds and sizzle for about 30 seconds until fragrant, then add the onion and stir-fry for 2–3 minutes until soft and translucent. Add the garlic and ginger and stir-fry for 1 minute. Add the spice paste and cook gently, stirring occasionally, for 2–3 minutes until fragrant.

3 Tip in the marinated chicken pieces and stir-fry for 5–7 minutes until they turn opaque. Stir in the tomatoes, then add the lime juice and 100ml/3½fl oz/generous ⅓ cup water and bring to the boil. Add the coconut milk, stir to combine and then bring to a gentle boil. Reduce the heat to low and simmer, covered, for 15–20 minutes until the sauce starts to thicken and the chicken is cooked through. Serve hot with the coriander sprinkled over and either boiled rice or Garlic Naan on the side.

tandoori chicken with garlic naan

This is one of the most popular dishes in Indian cuisine. The chicken is tenderized with yogurt, aromatic spices and roots, and a little red food colouring is added to give the trademark, bright red appearance. Here, however, I am using ground saffron to give it a slightly different edge. This well-flavoured chicken is especially good with naan bread, and I've included the recipe for Garlic Naan. If you prefer, you could replace the garlic with fresh herbs for a herb-flavoured naan.

SERVES 6
PREPARATION TIME 30 minutes,
  plus minimum 5 hours 30 minutes
  marinating and resting time
COOKING TIME about 1 hour
  15 minutes

TANDOORI CHICKEN
6 chicken legs, skin removed
5 tbsp yogurt
4 garlic cloves, grated
2cm/¾in piece of root ginger,
  peeled and grated
2 tsp chilli powder
1 tsp paprika
2 tsp ground cumin
2 tsp turmeric
1 tbsp ground coriander
½ tsp freshly ground black
  pepper
¼ tsp ground saffron
½ tsp sea salt
juice of ½ lime
1 tbsp sunflower oil
30g/1oz butter, softened
1 handful of coriander leaves,
  chopped, to serve
1 onion, sliced, to serve

1 Transfer the chicken legs to a chopping board and then, using a sharp knife, make 3 long, deep diagonal slits into the thigh area of the legs and 3 smaller ones into the drumsticks.

2 Put all the remaining tandoori chicken ingredients, except the butter, in a large bowl and mix well to make a paste. Add the chicken legs and rub the paste into the chicken until it is well coated. Cover with cling film and leave to marinate in the fridge for 5–6 hours or, for an even better flavour, overnight.

3 To make the naan dough, stir the sugar into 200ml/7fl oz/scant 1 cup water until dissolved. Sift the flour into a large mixing bowl and then mix in the yeast, baking powder, salt and garlic. Make a well in the centre and pour in the melted butter. Slowly pour in the water and combine with the other ingredients to form a soft dough. Add extra flour if the dough is too sticky. Turn the dough out onto a lightly floured surface and knead for 10 minutes until it is smooth and elastic. Place the dough back in the bowl, cover with a damp tea towel and leave to stand in a warm place for 1–1½ hours, or until the dough has doubled in size.

4 Turn the risen dough onto a lightly floured surface and divide into 2 portions. Knead each portion for 2 minutes, roll into a cylinder and divide into 5 equal pieces. Keeping the dough that you are not using covered with a damp tea towel, shape a dough piece into a ball and then flatten using your hand. Using a rolling pin, roll the dough into a 13cm/5in disc about 5mm/¼in thick. Put the disc on a floured tray, cover with a damp tea towel and repeat for the remaining dough balls.

GARLIC NAAN
1 tsp granulated sugar
350g/12oz/heaped 2¾ cups
   plain flour, plus extra for
   dusting
1 tsp dried active yeast
1 tsp baking powder
¼ tsp fine sea salt
6 garlic cloves, finely chopped
55g/2oz butter, melted, plus
   extra for greasing

TO SERVE
1 lime, cut into wedges

5 Heat a griddle pan or heavy-based frying pan over a high heat and grease with a little melted butter. Add a portion of dough and cook for 3–4 minutes on each side until it blisters and brown spots form. When cooked, melt a small knob of butter on both sides of the naan, then transfer it to a heatproof tray and keep warm. Repeat until all the naan are cooked.

6 Meanwhile, remove the marinated chicken from the fridge, pour off any excess liquid and leave to stand at room temperature for 25–30 minutes before cooking. Preheat the oven to 200°C/400°F/ Gas 6. Place a roasting rack on a baking tray and arrange the chicken legs on the rack. Smear some of the butter over each chicken leg, then put in the oven for 30–35 minutes until cooked through. When the tip of a sharp knife is inserted into the thickest part of the meat, the juices should run clear. Serve hot with the coriander and onion sprinkled over the top and the naan and lime wedges on the side.

DEVILLED PORK

In this Sri Lankan dish, the meat is slowly cooked in a well-flavoured sauce – the richness and depth of aromas develop and the tender meat melts in your mouth.

SERVES 4–6
PREPARATION TIME 20 minutes
COOKING TIME 1 hour
   25 minutes

2 tbsp sunflower oil
2 sprigs curry leaves
2 black cardamom pods
2 cloves
5cm/2in cinnamon stick
1 onion, chopped
2 green chillies, deseeded and
   halved
4 garlic cloves, finely chopped
2cm/¾in piece of root ginger,
   peeled and grated
1 tsp chilli powder
1 tsp turmeric
½ tsp ground cumin
1 tsp ground coriander
800g/1lb 12oz deboned pork
   shoulder, trimmed and cut
   into bite-sized pieces
2 tomatoes, skinned and
   roughly chopped (*see
   page 217*)
3 lemongrass stalks, outer
   leaves and stalk ends
   removed and crushed, or
   3 pandan leaves, tied into
   a knot
½ tsp sea salt
1 tbsp lime juice

TO SERVE
1 recipe quantity Boiled
   Long-Grain Rice
   (*see page 214*)

1 Heat the oil in a large, heavy-based saucepan over a medium-high heat. Add the curry leaves, cardamom pods, cloves and cinnamon stick and sizzle for a few seconds, then add the onion and stir-fry for 2–3 minutes until soft and translucent. Add the chillies, garlic and ginger and stir-fry for 1–2 minutes until fragrant. Add the chilli powder, turmeric, cumin and coriander and stir-fry for 1 minute. Tip in the pork, tomatoes, pandan leaves or lemongrass stalks and salt and toss until the pork is well coated with the spices.

2 Pour in the lime juice and 550ml/19fl oz/scant 2¼ cups water, increase the heat to high and bring to the boil. Cover the pan, reduce the heat to low and simmer for 1 hour 15 minutes, or until the pork is tender and the sauce has thickened, stirring occasionally. Serve hot with boiled rice.

kerala beef

Kerala is in South West India, and this is a great curry standby from the region, as it is can be whipped up quickly and then left on the hob to cook. The fresh coconut provides depth of flavour and also helps to thicken the sauce.

SERVES 4
PREPARATION TIME 35 minutes,
  plus 30 minutes marinating time
COOKING TIME about 45 minutes

500g/1lb 2oz beef fillet, cut
  into bite-sized pieces
3 garlic cloves, finely grated
5mm/¼in piece of root ginger,
  peeled and grated
1 tsp turmeric
¼ tsp freshly ground black
  pepper
2 tsp ground coriander
2 tsp ground cumin
2 tsp chilli powder
1 tbsp sunflower oil
1 onion, chopped
2 green bird's eye chillies,
  whole
2 sprigs curry leaves
1 tomato, skinned and roughly
  chopped (*see page 217*)
15g/½oz coconut flesh, thinly
  sliced (*see page 216*), or
  desiccated coconut, plus
  extra to serve
sea salt

TO SERVE
1 recipe quantity Boiled
  Long-Grain Rice
  (*see page 214*)

1 Put the beef in a bowl, add the garlic, ginger, turmeric, pepper, coriander, cumin and chilli powder and toss until the beef is well coated with the spices. Season with salt, then cover with cling film and leave to marinate for 30 minutes at room temperature.

2 Heat the oil in a heavy-based saucepan over a medium-high heat. Add the onion, chillies and curry leaves and stir-fry for 2–3 minutes until the onions are soft and translucent. Tip in the marinated beef, toss until the beef is well coated with all the other ingredients and cook for 5 minutes, stirring occasionally.

3 Add the tomato and coconut. Pour in 150ml/5fl oz/scant ⅔ cup water and stir well. Bring to the boil, then reduce the heat to low and simmer for 30–35 minutes until the beef is tender and the sauce starts to thicken, stirring occasionally. Serve warm with extra coconut sprinkled over and boiled rice.

Lamb rogan josh

Of Kashmir origin, Rogan Josh has become a favourite dish in both India and Pakistan. Very aromatic, there is no secret to this dish – the meat gets its flavour from the many spices used. The yogurt helps to tenderize the meat and is the base for the creamy sauce that coats the meat.

SERVES 4
PREPARATION TIME 15 minutes, plus minimum 2 hours marinating time
COOKING TIME about 1 hour

600g/1lb 5oz deboned lamb shoulder, trimmed and cut into bite-sized pieces
1 tsp chilli powder
1 tsp turmeric
100g/3½oz/scant ½ cup Greek yogurt
5 green cardamom pods
½ tsp black peppercorns
5–6 cloves
1 star anise
3cm/1¼in cinnamon stick
3–4 dried bay leaves
1 tbsp ground coriander
½ tbsp ground cumin
1 tbsp sunflower oil
2 onions, chopped
5 garlic cloves, finely chopped
3cm/1¼in piece of root ginger, peeled and grated
1 tbsp tomato purée
1 small handful of coriander leaves, to serve

TO SERVE
1 lime, cut into wedges
1 recipe quantity Boiled Long-Grain Rice (*see page 214*)

1 Put the lamb in a large bowl, then add the chilli powder, turmeric and yogurt and toss until all the pieces of lamb are well coated with the marinade. Cover with cling film and leave to marinate in the fridge for 2–3 hours or, for an even better flavour, overnight.

2 Put the cardamom pods, peppercorns, cloves, star anise, cinnamon stick and bay leaves in a food processor or coffee grinder and grind until powdery. Transfer the spices to a bowl and add the coriander and cumin. Heat a frying pan over a medium heat, then add the spice powder and dry-fry, stirring frequently, for 2–3 minutes until aromatic. Leave to one side to cool.

3 Heat the oil in a heavy-based saucepan over a medium heat. Add the spice powder and sizzle for a few seconds, then add the onions and stir-fry for 2–3 minutes until soft and translucent. Add the garlic and ginger and stir-fry for 1–2 minutes until fragrant. Tip in the marinated lamb, push around the pan until well coated with the spices, then cook for 15–20 minutes, or until the meat is sealed and browned, stirring occasionally.

4 Add 150ml/5fl oz/scant ⅔ cup water, bring to the boil for a few seconds, skim any fat or scum off the surface and add the tomato purée. Reduce the heat to low and simmer for 20–25 minutes until the meat is tender and almost falling apart. About 15 minutes into cooking, or when the pork becomes slightly dry, add another 100ml/3½fl oz/generous ⅓ cup water. Serve warm with the coriander sprinkled over, lime wedges on the side and boiled rice.

Lamb Korma

SERVES 4
PREPARATION TIME 15 minutes,
   plus 30 minutes marinating time
COOKING TIME about 2 hours
   15 minutes

700g/1lb 9oz deboned lamb
   shoulder, trimmed and cut
   into bite-sized pieces
1 tsp turmeric
2 tbsp sunflower oil
5cm/2in cinnamon stick
½ tsp black mustard seeds
2 cloves
3 green cardamom pods
2 star anise
3–4 black peppercorns
1 onion, roughly chopped
2cm/¾in piece of root ginger,
   peeled and grated
4 garlic cloves, finely chopped
2 red chillies, deseeded and
   halved lengthways
1 tsp ground coriander
½ tsp ground cumin
2 tomatoes, skinned and
   roughly chopped (*see page
   217*)
1 tbsp tomato purée
150ml/5fl oz/scant ⅔ cup
   coconut milk
½ tsp sea salt
200g/7oz butternut squash,
   deseeded, peeled and cut into
   wedges
1 handful of coriander leaves,
   chopped, to serve

TO SERVE
1 recipe quantity Boiled
   Long-Grain Rice, (*see page
   214*)

1 Put the lamb in a large bowl, then add the turmeric and toss until all the pieces of lamb are well coated with the spices. Cover with cling film and leave to marinate for 30 minutes at room temperature.

2 Heat the oil in a large saucepan over a medium heat. Add the cinnamon stick, mustard seeds, cloves, cardamom pods, star anise and peppercorns and sizzle for a few seconds until fragrant, then add the onion and stir-fry for 2–3 minutes until soft and translucent. Add the ginger, garlic and chillies and stir-fry for 2–3 minutes until fragrant, then add the coriander, cumin, tomatoes and tomato purée and mix well. Tip in the marinated lamb, toss until the lamb is well coated with all the other ingredients, then cook for 15–20 minutes until the meat is sealed and browned, stirring occasionally.

3 Add the coconut milk, salt and 500ml/17fl oz/2 cups water to the pan, mix well and bring to the boil. Reduce the heat to low and simmer, uncovered, for 30 minutes, then add the butternut squash and toss until well coated with the sauce. Simmer for a further 1 hour 15 minutes, or until the meat is tender. Serve hot with the coriander sprinkled over and boiled rice.

sour fish curry

This is a Sri Lankan speciality. An island nation, Sri Lanka is surrounded by the Indian Ocean where fish like tuna is abundant. Spices and fish go very well together, as the bolder touches of fragrant spices really complement the more subtle flavours of fish.

SERVES 4
PREPARATION TIME 10 minutes
COOKING TIME 15–25 minutes

2 tbsp sunflower oil
2 cloves
2 green cardamom pods
1 red onion, roughly chopped
2 sprigs curry leaves
1 recipe quantity Sour Fish Curry Spice Paste (*see page 209*)
1 tomato, skinned and roughly chopped (*see page 217*)
1 tbsp lime juice or ½ recipe quantity Tamarind Water (*see page 217*)
1 tbsp clear honey
500g/1lb 2oz boneless, skinless tuna or salmon steaks, cut into bite-sized pieces
sea salt

TO SERVE
1 recipe quantity Boiled Long-Grain Rice (*see page 214*)

1 Heat the oil in a heavy-based saucepan over a medium-high heat. Add the cloves and cardamom pods and sizzle for a few seconds, then add the onion and curry leaves and stir-fry for 2–3 minutes until the onion is soft and translucent. Add the spice paste and cook for 5–7 minutes until fragrant, stirring occasionally, then add the tomato and cook for a further 5 minutes.

2 Add the lime juice and 100ml/3½fl oz/generous ⅓ cup water and bring to the boil. Stir in the honey and tuna and season with salt, then reduce the heat to low and simmer, stirring occasionally, for 5–10 minutes until the fish is cooked through and the liquid has started to evaporate. Serve hot with boiled rice.

FISH curry WITH okra

Okra, also known as lady's fingers, are a great addition to curry dishes, because they go extremely well with spices. Raw, they have a crunchy texture, but when cooked the pods turn soft and gummy inside, and really soak up the flavours of the sauce.

SERVES 4
PREPARATION TIME 20 minutes
COOKING TIME 25 minutes

2 tbsp sunflower oil
¼ tsp black mustard seeds
3 sprigs curry leaves
1 red onion, sliced into rings
2 garlic cloves, finely chopped
1cm/½in piece of root ginger, peeled and finely grated
1 tsp ground coriander
½ tsp ground cumin
2 tsp chilli powder
½ tsp turmeric
½ tsp sea salt
1 tsp clear honey
1 tbsp lime juice
2 tomatoes, skinned and quartered (*see page 217*)
250ml/9fl oz/1 cup coconut milk
85g/3oz okra
2 mackerels, scaled and gutted by your fishmonger and cut into 3cm/1¼in steaks

TO SERVE
1 recipe quantity Boiled Long-Grain Rice (*see page 214*)

1 Heat the oil in a large saucepan over a medium-high heat. Add the mustard seeds and sizzle for a few seconds, then add the curry leaves and cook for 1 minute until fragrant. Add the onion, garlic and ginger and stir-fry for 2–3 minutes until fragrant and the onion is soft and translucent. Stir in the coriander, cumin, chilli powder, turmeric, salt, honey and lime juice, then add the tomatoes and mix well.

2 Pour the coconut milk and 60ml/2fl oz/¼ cup water into the pan and bring to the boil, then add the okra, reduce the heat to low, cover and simmer for 10–15 minutes until tender, stirring occasionally. Add the mackerel steaks and cook for 5 minutes, or until the flesh turns opaque, stirring occasionally. Serve hot with boiled rice.

prawn curry

If you love seafood you will love this Indian dish, which has mild but deep, aromatic flavours. The prawns are cooked unpeeled, adding an extra sweetness to the curry sauce, while the coconut milk adds a silkiness. If you prefer a spicy curry, replace the chilli powder in the spice paste with ground, dried chillies – a guaranteed spice kick!

SERVES 4
PREPARATION TIME 30 minutes
COOKING TIME 15–20 minutes

500g/1lb 2oz raw, unpeeled
  large king prawns
1 tbsp sunflower oil
¼ tsp black mustard seeds
2 sprigs curry leaves
1 onion, chopped
2 garlic cloves, finely chopped
1cm/½in piece of root ginger,
  peeled and finely chopped
1 tsp chilli powder
½ tsp turmeric
1 tsp ground coriander
¼ tsp cinnamon
½ tsp ground cumin
½ tsp sea salt
1 tsp granulated sugar
1 tbsp lime juice
200ml/7fl oz/scant 1 cup
  coconut milk
1 tbsp coriander leaves,
  to serve

TO SERVE
1 recipe quantity Boiled
  Long-Grain Rice
  (*see page 214*)

1 Heat the oil in a heavy-based saucepan over a medium-high heat. Add the black mustard seeds and sizzle for a few seconds, then add the curry leaves and cook for 1 minute until fragrant. Add the onion, garlic and ginger and stir-fry for 3–5 minutes until fragrant and the onion is soft and translucent.

2 Add the chilli powder, turmeric, coriander, cinnamon, cumin, salt, sugar and lime juice to the pan and stir until all the ingredients are well combined. Pour in the coconut milk and bring to the boil, then reduce the heat to low. Add the prawns, stirring until well coated with the sauce, then cover and simmer for 5–10 minutes until the prawns turn pink and are cooked through, stirring occasionally. Serve immediately with the coriander sprinkled over and boiled rice.

paneer & spinach curry

This is a hearty northern Indian dish that is flavoured with spices, and has a rich and creamy tomato and spinach based gravy. The mild Indian cheese is pan-fried to add some crispiness to its outer layer, then cooked and coated with the aromatic sauce. It is delicious and suitable for vegetarians.

SERVES 4
PREPARATION TIME 15 minutes
COOKING TIME 20–25 minutes

150g/5½oz baby leaf spinach
2 tbsp sunflower oil
250g/9oz paneer cheese, cubed
2 onions, chopped
2 green chillies, deseeded and halved lengthways
2 garlic cloves, finely chopped
1cm/½in piece of root ginger, peeled and grated
1 tsp ground coriander
1 tsp ground cumin
1 tsp turmeric
½ tsp chilli powder
3 tomatoes, skinned and roughly chopped (*see page 217*)
sea salt

TO SERVE
1 recipe quantity Boiled Long-Grain Rice (*see page 214*)

1 Bring a saucepan of water to the boil, add the spinach and blanch for 1 minute. Drain, squeezing out as much water as possible, then transfer the spinach to a food processor and blend to a smooth paste. Leave to one side.

2 Heat 1 tablespoon of the oil in a frying pan over a medium-high heat. Add the paneer and fry, stirring frequently, for 6–8 minutes until brown all round. Leave to one side.

3 Heat the remaining tablespoon of oil in a saucepan over a medium-high heat. Add the onions and chillies and stir-fry for 2–3 minutes until the onions are soft and translucent. Add the garlic and ginger and stir-fry for 1–2 minutes until fragrant, then stir in the coriander, cumin, turmeric and chilli powder. Add the tomatoes, spinach paste and 55ml/1¾fl oz/scant ¼ cup water and bring to the boil. Reduce the heat to low and simmer for 10 minutes, or until the sauce is thickened, stirring occasionally. Add the paneer, stir to combine with the sauce and season with salt. Serve hot with boiled rice.

cashew nut & coconut curry

Cashew nuts have a delicate flavour that complement all the different spices in this delicious curry and they also create a really smooth and creamy sauce. This dish is a genuine classic Sri Lankan dish that is served with other curries, and is usually included on the menu for special occasions.

SERVES 4–6
PREPARATION TIME 15 minutes
COOKING TIME about 45 minutes

1 tsp ground coriander
½ tsp ground cumin
1 tsp turmeric
2 tbsp sunflower oil
1 onion, chopped
2 lemongrass stalks, outer
  leaves and stalk ends
  removed and crushed, or
  2 pandan leaves, tied into
  a knot
5cm/2in cinnamon stick
2cm/¾in piece of root ginger,
  peeled and grated
3 garlic cloves, finely minced
1 tsp chilli powder
½ tsp freshly ground black
  pepper
300g/10½oz/scant 2 cups
  cashew nuts
350ml/12fl oz/scant 1½ cups
  coconut milk
1 tsp granulated sugar
1 tsp sea salt
1 handful of coriander leaves,
  chopped, to serve
1 handful of mint leaves,
  chopped, to serve

TO SERVE
1 recipe quantity Boiled
  Long-Grain Rice
  (*see page 214*)

1 Heat a heavy-based frying pan over a medium-high heat. Add the coriander, cumin and turmeric and dry-fry for 1–2 minutes until fragrant. Remove from the heat and leave to one side.

2 Heat the oil in a large saucepan over a medium-high heat. Add the onion and stir-fry for 2–3 minutes until soft and translucent. Tip in the lemongrass stalks and cinnamon stick and stir-fry for 1 minute, then add the ginger and garlic and stir-fry for 2 minutes, or until fragrant. Stir in the toasted spice powder, chilli powder and pepper, then toss through the cashew nuts until well coated with the spices.

3 Pour in the coconut milk and 115ml/3¾fl oz/scant ½ cup water. Bring to the boil, then reduce the heat to low, cover and simmer for 15 minutes, stirring occasionally.

4 Add the sugar and salt, stir to mix well, then continue to simmer for a further 15 minutes until the cashew nuts start to soften. Sprinkle over the coriander and mint and serve hot with boiled rice.

Aubergine curry

Aubergine is a great choice for a curry because, when cooked, it becomes very soft and tender. Its unique flavour goes particularly well in this recipe, as it acts like a sponge and absorbs the spicy sauce. If you can get them, baby aubergines, which are slim and oblong in shape, are great in this dish because of their softer texture when cooked.

SERVES 4
PREPARATION TIME 15 minutes, plus 30 minutes resting time
COOKING TIME 25 minutes

250g/9oz baby aubergines or large aubergine
2 tbsp sunflower oil
½ tsp black mustard seeds
1 onion, chopped
1 recipe quantity Aubergine Curry Spice Paste (*see page 206*)
100g/3½oz sweet potato, peeled and cut into small cubes
1 tbsp lime juice
sea salt

TO SERVE
Garlic Naan (*see page 180*)

1 Cut the baby aubergines in half lengthways or the large aubergine in slices about 1cm/½in thick, then arrange on a tray, cut sides facing up, and generously sprinkle with salt. Leave to stand for 30 minutes, then rinse under running cold water and pat dry with kitchen paper. Leave to one side.

2 Heat the oil in a large, deep, heavy-based frying pan. Add the mustard seeds and sizzle for a few seconds, then add the onion and stir-fry for 2–3 minutes until soft and translucent. Add the spice paste and cook gently, stirring occasionally, for 5–7 minutes until fragrant.

3 Tip the aubergine and sweet potato into the pan, toss until well coated with the paste, then cook, stirring occasionally, for 5 minutes until they start to soften. Add the lime juice and 55ml/1¾fl oz/ scant ¼ cup water and season with salt. Reduce the heat to low and cook, covered, for 10 minutes until the aubergine and sweet potato are soft. Serve hot with the Garlic Naan.

masala dosa

My love of Indian food started when I was eight years old and my mum served me my first Roti Canai (*see page 112*). One of my all-time favourites now is Masala Dosa – crispy roti wrapped with masala squash and served with any kind of curry sauce and chutney you like.

MAKES about 8
PREPARATION TIME 20 minutes, plus soaking the dhal and rice overnight and 3–4 hours fermenting time
COOKING TIME 30–45 minutes

1 tbsp sunflower oil, plus extra for oiling
½ tsp black mustard seeds
2 sprigs curry leaves
1 small butternut squash, deseeded, peeled and diced
2 carrots, diced
½ tsp ground coriander
¼ tsp ground cumin
½ tsp turmeric
¼ tsp chilli powder
sea salt and freshly ground black pepper

DOSA
80g/2¾oz/½ cup split white or black urad dahl, washed and soaked overnight
150g/5½oz/¾ cup basmati rice, washed and soaked overnight
¼ tsp chilli powder

TO SERVE
Dhal Curry (*see page 112 – optional*)
Sambal (*see page 213*)
plain yogurt

1 To make the dosa batter, drain and rinse the soaked urad dahl and basmati rice under running cold water, drain again and put in a food processor or blender. Blitz for a few seconds, then gradually pour in 290ml/10fl oz/generous 1 cup water until a smooth paste forms. Transfer the mixture to a bowl, add the chilli powder and season with salt and pepper. Cover with cling film and leave to stand at room temperature for 3–4 hours for the batter to ferment.

2 Heat the oil in a frying pan over a medium-high heat. Add the mustard seeds and curry leaves and sizzle for a few seconds, then add the butternut squash and carrots and cook, stirring occasionally, for 7–8 minutes until they start to soften. Add the coriander, cumin, turmeric and chilli powder and season with salt and pepper. Pour 150ml/5fl oz/scant ⅔ cup water into the pan and bring to the boil. Reduce the heat to low and cook, covered, for 15–20 minutes until the squash and carrots are softened. Set aside and keep warm.

3 Meanwhile, pour some oil into a large, non-stick frying pan or crêpe pan over a medium-high heat, then use kitchen paper to grease the pan evenly and soak up any excess oil. When the pan is hot, ladle about 55ml/1¾fl oz/scant ¼ cup of the dosa batter into the pan and use the base of the ladle to spread the mixture out as evenly as possible, using a circular motion, until about 23cm/9in in diameter. Cook for 2–3 minutes on each side until golden brown and crisp around the edges.

4 Transfer the dosa to a clean surface and put 2–3 tablespoons of the butternut squash mixture in the centre and mould into an oblong shape. Fold the dosa in half over the mixture, then transfer to a serving plate and keep warm. Repeat until all the batter is used. Serve immediately with Dhal Curry, Sambal and yogurt if you like.

BEEF & VEGETABLE ROTI PARCELS

MAKES 14
PREPARATION TIME 30 minutes,
plus 1 hour resting time
COOKING TIME about 1 hour

200g/7oz sweet potatoes,
    diced
150g/5½oz floury potatoes,
    diced
1 tbsp sunflower oil, plus extra
    for oiling
1 onion, finely chopped
1 sprig curry leaves, finely
    chopped
1 tsp ground cumin
1 tsp ground coriander
½ tsp chilli powder
¼ tsp turmeric
1 small carrot, cut into
    matchsticks
2 spring onions, finely
    chopped
250g/9oz beef mince
sea salt and freshly ground
    black pepper

ROTI DOUGH
½ tsp sea salt
250g/9oz/2 cups plain flour
1 tbsp sunflower oil, plus extra
    for kneading and oiling

TO SERVE
chilli sauce (optional)

1 To make the roti dough, dissolve the salt in 150ml/5fl oz/scant
   ⅔ cup water. Put the flour in a large mixing bowl, make a well in
   the centre and add the oil. Slowly pour in the salted water and
   combine with the other ingredients to form a soft dough. Knead for
   10 minutes, or until the dough is smooth and elastic, then shape
   into a ball. Cover with cling film and leave to stand at room
   temperature for about 30 minutes.

2 Bring a saucepan of well-salted water to the boil. Tip in both the
   sweet and floury potatoes and cook for 10–15 minutes until soft.
   Drain well, then roughly mash with a fork and set aside.

3 Meanwhile, heat the oil in a frying pan over a medium-high heat.
   Add the onion and stir-fry for 2–3 minutes until soft and
   translucent. Add the curry leaves, cumin, coriander, chilli powder
   and turmeric and stir-fry for about 1 minute. Add the carrot and
   spring onions and cook for 5 minutes, or until the carrots are tender,
   stirring occasionally. Add the beef mince, break up any lumps and
   then add 2 tablespoons water. Season with salt and pepper, then
   cook for 5–7 minutes until cooked through, stirring occasionally.
   Stir in the mashed potatoes, then remove the pan from the heat and
   leave to one side.

4 Turn the dough onto a lightly oiled surface and knead for 5 minutes.
   Divide the dough into 14 portions and shape each into a ball. Brush
   the balls generously with oil, then place side by side on a well-oiled
   dish. Cover with cling film and leave to stand at room temperature
   for 30 minutes.

5 Oil a clean working surface and generously oil your palms. Take a
   dough ball and flatten, then slowly work the dough outwards from
   around the edge until the circle is about 14–16cm/5½–6¼in in
   diameter. Place 2 tablespoons of the potato mixture in the centre
   of the pastry, slightly flatten the mixture and mould into an oblong
   shape about 1.5cm/⅝in thick. Fold the bottom edge of the pastry
   over the filling, fold in the two sides and roll up tightly. Transfer to
   a lightly oiled plate and repeat until all the dough balls are used.

6 Lightly oil a large, non-stick frying pan and place over a medium-
   high heat. Fry 4–5 rotis at a time for 8–10 minutes until crisp and
   brown all round, then turn the rotis upright and fry each end for
   2–3 minutes until brown spots form. Remove from the pan and
   keep warm. Repeat until all the rotis are cooked. Serve hot with
   chilli sauce on the side, if you like.

sri Lankan crispy pancakes

Hoppers, also known as Appam, are eaten in Sri Lanka at breakfast, lunch and dinner. They are cooked in a special pan that looks like a mini wok, giving them a curvy shape when cooked. If you don't have a hopper pan, you can improvise by using either a small non-stick frying pan or the bottom section of a wok. Hoppers can be made in a variety of different ways, both sweet and savoury, and the egg hopper is one very popular example. Here I have included a recipe for a plain hopper, but I have included instructions on how to make simple sweet hoppers and egg hoppers, too. Because of their simple flavour and crispy outer layer, plain hoppers are great with curries.

MAKES 12
PREPARATION TIME 10 minutes, plus 2 hours resting time
COOKING TIME about 1 hour

PLAIN HOPPERS
2 tsp granulated sugar
½ tsp sea salt
2¼ tsp dried active yeast
500ml/17fl oz/2 cups coconut milk
350g/12oz/2 cups rice flour
2 eggs
sunflower oil, for oiling

SWEET HOPPERS
granulated or soft light brown sugar, to taste
shredded fresh coconut or desiccated coconut, to taste

EGG HOPPERS
12 eggs

1 Mix the sugar, salt and yeast in the coconut milk until dissolved. Put the rice flour in a large mixing bowl, make a well in the centre and crack the eggs into the well. Gradually add the coconut milk mixture, whisking continuously to form a smooth batter. Cover with cling film and leave to stand in a warm place for 2 hours.

2 Pour some oil into a hopper pan or 16cm/6¼in heavy-based frying pan over a medium-high heat, then use kitchen paper to grease the pan evenly and soak up any excess oil. When the pan is hot, ladle about 80ml/2½fl oz/⅓ cup of the batter into the centre of the pan and quickly lift and swirl the pan to form a thin layer over the base and as far up the sides of the pan as possible to create a bowl shape. Cover the pan, reduce the heat to medium and cook for 3–4 minutes until the edges start to brown and bubbles start to form on the surface. The pancake should be crispy on the outside and slightly spongy in the middle. Transfer the hopper to a serving plate and keep warm, then repeat until all the batter is used.

3 To make sweet hoppers, sprinkle sugar and coconut, to taste, over the plain hopper halfway through cooking. Serve immediately.

4 To make egg hoppers, crack an egg into the centre of each hopper after 1–2 minutes of cooking or when the batter starts to thicken and set. Continue to cook, still covered, for 1–2 minutes until the egg white turns solid and opaque. Serve immediately.

Basic recipes

Within the main recipes you will often find cross-references to spice pastes, condiments, rice and noodles that will be either a key part of the recipe or a suggested accompaniment to the dish. All the recipes, including my fool-proof method to boil rice, can be found here. Each paste recipe makes the exact quantity you will need in the recipe, and takes 5–10 minutes to make, plus any soaking time required. A mortar and pestle can be used instead of a food processor to blend the pastes, if you prefer.

SPICE PASTES

Aubergine curry spice paste

3 dried chillies • 2 red chillies, deseeded and roughly chopped • 3 garlic cloves, roughly chopped • 5 shallots, roughly chopped • 1cm/½in piece of root ginger, peeled and roughly chopped • ¼ tsp turmeric • ½ tsp ground coriander • ½ tsp ground cumin

1 Soak the dried chillies in hot water for 10 minutes, then drain, deseed and roughly chop. Put all the chillies, garlic, shallots and ginger in a food processor and blend into a smooth paste. Add the turmeric, coriander and cumin and mix well.

Assam laksa spice paste

4 dried chillies • 6 red chillies, deseeded and roughly chopped • 1 tsp roasted shrimp paste (*see page 217*) • 10 shallots, roughly chopped • 1 lemongrass stalk, outer leaves and stalk end removed and roughly chopped

1 Soak the dried chillies in hot water for 10 minutes, then drain, deseed and roughly chop. Put all the ingredients in a food processor and blend to a smooth paste.

Ayam masak merah spice paste

3 dried chillies • 10 shallots, roughly chopped • 4 garlic cloves, roughly chopped • 2cm/¾in piece of root ginger, peeled and roughly chopped • 3 red chillies, deseeded and roughly chopped

1 Soak the dried chillies in hot water for 10 minutes, then drain, deseed and roughly chop. Put all the ingredients in a food processor and blend to a smooth paste.

Chilli crab spice paste

2 dried chillies • 5 red chillies, deseeded and roughly chopped • 2 garlic cloves, roughly chopped • 6 shallots, roughly chopped • 5cm/2in piece of root ginger, peeled and roughly chopped • 1 tsp roasted shrimp paste (*see page 217*)

1 Soak the dried chillies in hot water for 10 minutes, then drain, deseed and roughly chop. Put all the ingredients in a food processor and blend to a smooth paste.

coorg-style curry spice paste

2 green chillies, deseeded and roughly chopped • 1 red onion, roughly chopped • 3 garlic cloves, roughly chopped • 1cm/½in piece of root ginger, peeled and roughly chopped • ¼ tsp black peppercorns • ½ tsp ground cumin • 1 tsp ground coriander

1 Put all the ingredients, except the cumin and coriander, in a food processor and blend to a smooth paste. Add the cumin and coriander and mix well.

coto makassar spice paste

3 green chillies, deseeded and roughly chopped • 2 red chillies, deseeded and roughly chopped • 3cm/1¼in piece of root ginger, peeled and roughly chopped • 3 garlic cloves, roughly chopped • 80g/2¾oz coriander leaves, roughly chopped • 1 tsp ground coriander • ½ tsp ground turmeric

1 Put all the ingredients, except the ground coriander and turmeric, in a food processor and blend to a smooth paste. Add the coriander and turmeric and mix well.

curry fish mousse spice paste

1 red chilli, deseeded and roughly chopped • 2 garlic cloves, roughly chopped • 5 shallots, roughly chopped • 2 lemongrass stalks, outer leaves and stalk ends removed and roughly chopped • 1cm/½in piece of fresh turmeric, peeled and roughly chopped, or ½ tsp ground turmeric • 2cm/¾in piece of galangal, peeled and roughly chopped • 2 kaffir lime leaves, roughly chopped

1 Put all the ingredients, except the ground turmeric, if using, in a food processor and blend to a smooth paste. Add the ground turmeric and mix well.

gado gado spice paste

3 red chillies, deseeded and roughly chopped • 3 garlic cloves, roughly chopped • 5 shallots, roughly chopped • 2cm/¾in piece of root ginger, peeled and roughly chopped • 1 lemongrass stalk, outer leaves and stalk end removed and roughly chopped • 1 tsp roasted shrimp paste (*see page 217*)

1 Blend all the ingredients in a food processor to a smooth paste.

kare kare spice paste

2 red chillies, deseeded and roughly chopped • 4 garlic cloves, roughly chopped • 8 shallots, roughly chopped • 2cm/¾in piece of root ginger, peeled and roughly chopped • 1 tsp roasted shrimp paste (*see page 217*)

1 Blend all the ingredients in a food processor to a smooth paste.

KHMER YELLOW CURRY SPICE PASTE

1 red chilli, deseeded and roughly chopped • 4 garlic cloves, roughly chopped • 5 shallots, roughly chopped • 2 lemongrass stalks, outer leaves and stalk ends removed and roughly chopped • 3 kaffir lime leaves, roughly chopped • 2cm/¾in piece of galangal, peeled and roughly chopped • 2cm/¾in piece of fresh turmeric, peeled and roughly chopped, or 1 tsp ground turmeric

1 Put all the ingredients, except the ground turmeric, if using, in a food processor and blend to a smooth paste. Add the ground turmeric and mix well.

LAKSA SPICE PASTE

10 dried chillies • 5 red chillies, deseeded and roughly chopped • 6 garlic cloves, roughly chopped • 18 shallots, roughly chopped • 1 lemongrass stalk, outer leaves and stalk end removed and roughly chopped • 2cm/¾in piece of root ginger, peeled and roughly chopped • 1 tsp roasted shrimp paste (*see page 217*) • 2 macadamia nuts • 4cm/1½in piece of fresh turmeric, peeled and roughly chopped, or 2 tsp ground turmeric • 1 tbsp ground coriander • 1 tsp ground cumin

1 Soak the dried chillies in hot water for 10 minutes, then drain, deseed and roughly chop. Put all the ingredients, except the ground turmeric, if using, coriander and cumin, in a food processor and blend to a smooth paste. Add the ground turmeric, coriander and cumin and mix well.

PAJERI NANAS SPICE PASTE

3 dried chillies • 6 red chillies, deseeded and roughly chopped • 3 garlic cloves, roughly chopped • 10 shallots, roughly chopped • 1cm/½in piece of root ginger, peeled and roughly chopped

1 Soak the dried chillies in hot water for 10 minutes, then drain, deseed and roughly chop. Put all the ingredients in a food processor and blend to a smooth paste.

PANANG CURRY SPICE PASTE

8 dried chillies • 2 red chillies, deseeded and roughly chopped • 1 tsp roasted shrimp paste (*see page 217*) • 2 garlic cloves, roughly chopped • 4 shallots, roughly chopped • 1 lemongrass stalk, outer leaves and stalk end removed and roughly chopped • 3cm/1¼in piece of galangal, peeled and roughly chopped • 2 kaffir lime leaves, roughly chopped • 2 coriander roots with stalks, roughly chopped • 1 tsp ground coriander • ½ tsp ground cumin

1 Soak the dried chillies in hot water for 10 minutes, then drain, deseed and roughly chop. Put all the ingredients, except the ground coriander and cumin, in a food processor and blend to a smooth paste. Add the coriander and cumin to the paste and mix well.

RENDANG SPICE PASTE

8 dried chillies • 4 red chillies, deseeded and roughly chopped • 5 garlic cloves, roughly chopped • 1 red onion, roughly chopped • 10 shallots, roughly chopped • 1 lemongrass stalk, outer leaves and stalk end removed and roughly chopped • 2cm/¾in piece of root ginger, peeled and roughly chopped • 2cm/¾in piece of galangal, peeled and roughly chopped • 2cm/¾in piece of fresh turmeric, peeled and roughly chopped, or 1 tsp ground turmeric • 1 tbsp ground coriander • 1 tsp ground cumin

1 Soak the dried chillies in hot water for 10 minutes, then drain, deseed and roughly chop. Put all the ingredients, except the ground turmeric, if using, coriander and cumin, in a food processor and blend to a smooth paste. Add the ground turmeric, coriander and cumin and mix well.

SATE LILIT IKAN SPICE PASTE

5 red chillies, deseeded and roughly chopped • 4 garlic cloves, roughly chopped • 8 shallots, roughly chopped • 3cm/1¼in piece of root ginger, peeled and roughly chopped • 1 lemongrass stalk, outer leaves and stalk end removed and roughly chopped • 3 kaffir lime leaves, roughly chopped • 2 macadamia nuts • 1 tsp roasted shrimp paste (*see page 217*) • 1cm/½in piece of fresh turmeric, peeled and roughly chopped, or ½ tsp ground turmeric • 1 tsp ground coriander

1 Put all the ingredients, except the ground turmeric, if using, and coriander in a food processor and blend to a smooth paste. Add the ground turmeric and coriander and mix well.

SOUR FISH CURRY SPICE PASTE

½ tsp turmeric • ½ tsp ground coriander • ½ tsp chilli powder • ¼ tsp ground cumin • ¼ tsp freshly ground black pepper • 3 shallots, roughly chopped • 2 garlic cloves, roughly chopped • 3 green chillies, deseeded and roughly chopped • 1cm/½in piece of root ginger, peeled and roughly chopped

1 Put the turmeric, coriander, chilli powder, cumin and black pepper in a frying pan over a medium-high heat and dry-fry for 1–2 minutes until fragrant and slightly smoky. Transfer to a mixing bowl. Put the shallots, garlic, green chillies and ginger in a food processor and blend to a smooth paste. Add the toasted spice powder and mix well.

SQUID SPICE PASTE

4 dried chillies • 5 red chillies, deseeded and roughly chopped • 3 garlic cloves, roughly chopped • 10 shallots, roughly chopped • 1 tsp roasted shrimp paste (*see page 217*) • 2 macadamia nuts

1 Soak the dried chillies in hot water for 10 minutes, then drain, deseed and roughly chop. Put all the ingredients in a food processor and blend to a smooth paste.

THAI green curry spice paste

7 green chillies, deseeded and roughly chopped • 2 red bird's eye chillies, deseeded and roughly chopped • 5 shallots, roughly chopped • 3 garlic cloves, roughly chopped • 3cm/1¼in piece of galangal, peeled and roughly chopped • 1 lemongrass stalk, outer leaves and stalk end removed and roughly chopped • 3 kaffir lime leaves, roughly chopped • 1 tsp roasted shrimp paste (*see page 217*) • 3 coriander roots with stalks and leaves, roughly chopped • 5mm/¼in piece of fresh turmeric, peeled and roughly chopped, or ¼ tsp ground turmeric

1 Put all the ingredients, except the ground turmeric, if using, in a food processor and blend to a smooth paste. Add the ground turmeric and mix well.

THAI roast chicken spice paste

1 red chilli, deseeded and roughly chopped • 3 shallots, roughly chopped • 1 lemongrass stalk, outer leaves and stalk end removed and roughly chopped • 2 coriander roots with stalks, roughly chopped • 2cm/¾in piece of fresh turmeric, peeled and roughly chopped, or 1 tsp ground turmeric

1 Put all the ingredients, except the ground turmeric, if using, in a food processor and blend to a smooth paste. Add the ground turmeric and mix well.

THAI red curry spice paste

8 dried chillies • 2 red chillies, deseeded and roughly chopped • 2 garlic cloves, roughly chopped • 4 shallots, roughly chopped • ½ lemongrass stalk, outer leaves and stalk end removed and roughly chopped • 3cm/1¼in piece of galangal, peeled and roughly chopped • 1 tsp roasted shrimp paste (*see page 217*) • 2 coriander roots with stalks, roughly chopped • 2 kaffir lime leaves, roughly chopped

1 Soak the dried chillies in hot water for 10 minutes, then drain, deseed and roughly chop. Put all the ingredients in a food processor and blend to a smooth paste.

STOCKS

CHICKEN STOCK

800g/1lb 12oz chicken wings and drumsticks, skin and excess fat removed, or 1 x 1.5kg/3lb 5 oz chicken carcass • 5cm/2in piece of root ginger, peeled and finely chopped • 6 spring onions, cut in half lengthways • 5 garlic cloves, chopped • ¼ tsp white peppercorns • 1 star anise • 2 tbsp Shaoxing rice wine

1 Put the chicken, ginger, spring onions, garlic, white peppercorns, star anise and rice wine in a large saucepan over a medium-high heat. Add 2 litres/ 70fl oz/8 cups water and bring to the boil. Reduce the heat to low, cover and simmer for 2–3 hours, skimming off any scum from the surface as required.
2 Remove the pan from the heat and discard all the solid ingredients. Cool the stock, then strain over a bowl lined with muslin. Chicken stock can be frozen for up to 1 month.

PORK STOCK

300g/10½oz chicken wings and drumsticks, skin and excess fat removed • 500g/1lb 2oz pork ribs or pork bones • 5cm/2in piece of root ginger, peeled and finely chopped • 3 spring onions, cut in half lengthways • 5 garlic cloves, finely chopped • ¼ tsp white peppercorns

1 Put the chicken pieces, pork ribs, ginger, spring onions, garlic, white peppercorns and 2 litres/70fl oz/8 cups water in a large saucepan and bring to the boil. Reduce the heat to low and simmer for 2–3 hours, skimming off any scum from the surface as required.
2 Remove the pan from the heat and discard all the solid ingredients. Cool the stock, then strain over a bowl lined with muslin. Pork stock can be frozen for up to 1 month.

DASHI

12cm/4½in kombu • 25g/1oz dried bonito flakes

1 Wipe the kombu with damp kitchen paper to remove any powder residue. Put the kombu in a saucepan and add 1.25 litres/44fl oz/5 cups water. Leave to sit for 30 minutes. Place the saucepan over a medium-low heat, bring to the boil and then remove the kombu. Reduce the heat to low, add the bonito flakes, cover and simmer for about 5 minutes.
2 Remove the pan from the heat and let the bonito flakes sink to the bottom. Skim off any scum from the surface, then strain the stock over a bowl lined with muslin. Leave the dashi to cool. This is Ichiban Dashi, which is the first stock with a more intense flavour.
3 You can reuse the kombu and bonito flakes to make Niban Dashi, which is the second stock with a milder flavour. Use the same amount of water as above and simmer all the ingredients for about 10 minutes. Strain the stock through muslin as above and discard the solids. Dashi can be frozen for up to 1 month.

CONDIMENTS & SIDES

CHILLI OIL

300ml/10½fl oz/scant 1¼ cups sunflower oil • 1 cinnamon stick, about 5cm/2in long • 1 star anise • 150g/5½oz/¾ cup chilli flakes • 1 tsp Sichuan peppercorns, crushed

1 Heat the oil in a deep, heavy-based frying pan to about 160°C/315°F or until a small piece of bread turns brown in 25–30 seconds. Add the cinnamon stick and star anise and fry for 1–2 minutes, stirring occasionally, until fragrant. Remove and discard the cinnamon stick and star anise.
2 Make sure the oil is still hot, but no hotter, and add the chilli flakes. Stir for a few seconds, then remove the pan from the heat.
3 Leave the oil and chilli flakes to cool and then transfer to a sterilized preserving jar or bottle. The chilli oil can be kept in the fridge for many weeks.

CHILLI PASTE

50g/1¾oz dried chillies • 3 tbsp sunflower oil • 1 tbsp sugar • ½ tsp salt

1 Soak the dried chillies in hot water for 10–15 minutes, then drain, deseed and roughly chop. Put the chillies in a food processor and blend to a smooth paste.
2 Heat the oil in a frying pan over a medium-high heat. Add the chilli paste and cook gently, stirring occasionally, for 15–20 minutes until fragrant and the oil starts to rise to the surface. Stir in the sugar and salt, remove from the heat and cool. Chilli paste can be frozen for up to 2 months.

FRIED SHALLOTS

250ml/9fl oz/1 cup sunflower oil • 350g/12oz red shallots, thinly sliced

1 Heat the oil in a frying pan over a medium heat. Insert a chopstick into the oil to test if it is hot enough – bubbles will start to form around the chopstick. Add the shallots and fry, stirring occasionally, for about 5–7 minutes until golden brown. Using a slotted spoon, remove the shallots from the pan and drain in a fine sieve over a mixing bowl, then on kitchen paper to soak up any excess oil.
2 Reuse the oil for cooking, if you like. Cool, then store in an airtight container in a cool, dark place for later use for up to 1 week.

GROUND TOASTED SICHUAN PEPPER

50g/1¾oz/¼ cup Sichuan peppercorns

1 Heat a frying pan over a medium-low heat. Add the Sichuan peppercorns and dry-fry for 5 minutes, or until fragrant – be careful they don't burn.
2 Remove from the heat and leave to cool. Grind the peppercorns in a food processor or coffee grinder and store in a cool, dark place in an airtight jar for up to 1 month.

NAM PRIK PAO

50g/1¾oz dried chillies, rinsed • 30g/1oz dried shrimps, rinsed • 125ml/4fl oz/½ cup sunflower oil • 30g/1oz garlic cloves, sliced • 100g/3½oz shallots, sliced • 1 tsp roasted shrimp paste (*see page 217*) • 2 tbsp fish sauce • 1 recipe quantity Tamarind Water (*see page 217*)

1 Heat a frying pan over a medium-high heat. Add the dried chillies and dry-fry for 2–3 minutes until slightly smoky. Remove from the pan and set aside. Make sure your kitchen is well ventilated because the smell can be very pungent.
2 Using the same pan, lightly fry the dried shrimps for 2–3 minutes until fragrant and the colour changes. Leave to one side to cool.
3 Meanwhile, heat the oil in a deep frying pan or wok over a medium heat. Add the garlic and shallots and fry, stirring occasionally, for 5–7 minutes until lightly golden brown. Using a slotted spoon, remove the shallots and garlic from the oil. Leave the frying pan, with the oil, for later use.
4 Once the shallots and garlic are cool, put in a food processor with the dried chillies, toasted dried shrimps and roasted shrimp paste and blend to a slightly coarse paste.

5 Reheat the oil in the frying pan over a medium-low heat. Add the chilli paste and cook gently, stirring occasionally, for 5 minutes, or until fragrant and the colour has darkened. Mix in the fish sauce and tamarind water. Transfer the paste to a preserving jar and cool. Store in the fridge for up to 1 month.

NUOC CHAM DIPPING SAUCE

1 garlic clove, finely chopped • 1 tsp chopped red bird's eye chilli • 2 tbsp caster sugar • 5 tbsp lime juice • 2 tbsp fish sauce

1 Put all the ingredients in a bowl, add 2 tablespoons water and stir until the sugar is dissolved.

PICKLED ginger

500g/1lb 2oz root ginger • 1 tbsp salt • 350ml/12fl oz/scant 1½ cups rice vinegar • 250g/9oz/scant 1¼ cups granulated sugar

1 Cut the ginger into small pieces for easier handling. Hold the ginger firmly in one hand and scrap off the peel using a spoon or a small, sharp knife. Slice the ginger into thin 2mm/¹⁄₁₆in pieces.
2 Put the ginger in a colander and rub with the salt to draw out the moisture. Leave to sit in the colander for about 1 hour, then rinse thoroughly under running cold water. Squeeze out any excess liquid and pat dry with kitchen paper. Transfer the ginger to a large preserving jar.
3 Put the rice vinegar and sugar in a saucepan over a medium-high heat. Bring to the boil, stirring continuously until the sugar is dissolved. Pour the liquid over the ginger and leave it to cool.
4 Cover and refrigerate for 24–36 hours before using. Pickled ginger can be stored in the fridge for up to 1 month.

SAMBAL

2 tsp roasted shrimp paste (*see page 217*) • 5 red chillies, deseeded and roughly chopped • 3 green bird's eye chillies, deseeded and roughly chopped • 2 tsp sugar • juice of 1 lime • ¼ tsp salt

1 Put the roasted shrimp paste and chillies in a food processor and blend to a smooth paste. Transfer to a mixing bowl, add the sugar, lime juice and salt and stir until the sugar is dissolved. Keep in a preserving jar in the fridge for up to 1 week.

SAMBAL MATAH

1 tsp roasted shrimp paste (*see page 217*) • 5 shallots, finely sliced • 2 garlic cloves, finely chopped • 2 red bird's eye chillies, deseeded and finely chopped • 2 kaffir lime leaves, finely chopped • 2 tsp sugar • 2 tbsp lime juice • a pinch of salt

1 Put all the ingredients in a bowl and mix until the sugar is dissolved and the paste well combined.

RICE

BOILED RICE

300g/10½oz/heaped 1⅓ cups short-grain rice or 350g/12oz/1¾ cups long-grain rice, such as jasmine and basmati

1 Put the rice in a large saucepan and pour in enough water to half fill the pan. Swirl the rice using your hand, lightly rubbing the grains, until the water is cloudy. Carefully pour off the water and repeat this process 3 or 4 times until the water is almost clear.

For Boiled Short-Grain Rice

2 Drain the rice into a sieve and leave to sit over a bowl for about 10 minutes, then transfer the rice to the saucepan and add 350ml/ 12fl oz/scant 1½ cups water. Leave to one side for about 20 minutes, then bring to the boil over a high heat and give it a quick stir. Reduce the heat to low, cover with a tight-fitting lid and simmer gently for about 15 minutes, or until the liquid is absorbed.

3 Remove the pan from the heat and then, using a wooden or plastic spatula, quickly loosen the grains. Replace the lid and leave the rice to steam for 15 minutes until fluffy.

For Boiled Long-Grain Rice

2 Cover the rice with water and leave to stand for 30 minutes. Drain the rice into a sieve and leave to sit over a bowl for 10 minutes, then transfer the rice to a saucepan and add 455ml/16fl oz/scant 2 cups water. Place the pan over a high heat and bring to the boil for about 20 seconds. Stir the rice with a wooden spoon to prevent the rice sticking to the base of the pan and then reduce the heat to low, cover and simmer gently for 20 minutes.

3 Remove the pan from the heat, leaving the lid tightly closed, and leave to steam for 10–15 minutes until the rice is cooked. Fluff the rice with a fork and keep warm.

BASIC TECHNIQUES

COOKING EGG AND RICE NOODLES AND RICE STICKS

1 Prepare a large bowl of ice-cold water and place it next to the hob. Fill a large saucepan with plenty of water and bring to the boil, then add the noodles or rice sticks and cook for the following times;

Fresh egg noodles   blanch for 25–30 seconds to warm through

Dried egg noodles   cook for 3–4 minutes until 'al dente'

Rice sticks   cook for 2–3 minutes until 'al dente'

Dried rice vermicelli   cook for 2–3 minutes until 'al dente'

Thick rice noodles   soak in boiling water for 30–45 minutes, then cook for 4–5 minutes until 'al dente'

2 Using a noodle skimmer or kitchen tongs, remove the cooked noodles from the water and plunge for a few seconds into the ice-cold water. Meanwhile, bring the water in the pan back to the boil. Return the noodles to the boiling water for a few seconds to warm through, then drain and continue according to the recipe instructions.

COOKING SOBA NOODLES

1 Bring plenty of water to the boil in a large saucepan, add the soba noodles and cook for about 3–4 minutes or until al dente. If unsure if they are ready, take a bite from a strand of noodle – it should be cooked through completely without a hard core.
2 Drain the noodles and rinse under running cold water, swirling and gently rubbing the strands to remove the starch. Continue rinsing until the water runs clear.
3 Meanwhile, bring another saucepan of water to the boil. Plunge the cooked and rinsed soba noodles into the water for a few seconds to heat through, then drain and continue according to the recipe instructions.

DEBONING CHICKEN LEGS

1 Rinse the chicken legs under running cold water and pat dry with kitchen paper. Place one leg, skin-side down, on a chopping board and cut through the joint between the thigh and the drumstick using a large, sharp knife.
2 Take the thigh and make an incision along the top of the bone. Using quick, short strokes, deepen the incision to cut the meat away from the bone. Pull clear the top part of the bone and then continue to make a few more cuts to remove the bone completely. Cut off any small bits of bone, tendons, fat and skin.
3 Use the same process to remove the bone from the drumstick. Repeat for the remaining legs.

FRESHLY GRATED COCONUT

1 Insert a sharp metal skewer into the 'eyes' at the bottom of the coconut and drain out the juice. Preheat the oven to 180°C/350°F/Gas 4 and bake the coconut for about 15 minutes. Remove from the oven and leave to one side until cool enough to handle.

2 Using a hammer or cleaver, tap the middle of the coconut until cracks forms, then break the coconut in two. If you have a coconut grater, use it to grate the coconut. If not, carefully slip a small, sharp knife between the shell and the flesh and pull the flesh away. Peel the brown skin off the back of the flesh using a vegetable peeler, then cut the flesh in chunks. Grate the flesh using a hand-held grater or blend it in a food processor to a desiccated coconut consistency.

FRESH COCONUT MILK

1 Grate the flesh, as above, and mix with 200ml/7fl oz/scant 1 cup water. Strain over a bowl lined with muslin, squeezing out as much milk as possible. This is the 'first press'. It is thick and concentrated and is sometimes known as coconut cream. Set the milk aside while you extract the 'second press' coconut milk.

2 Add 45ml/1½fl oz/3 tbsp water to the grated coconut in the muslin and strain over a separate bowl, squeezing out as much milk as possible. It will have a much thinner consistency.

3 Unless a recipe specifically asks for coconut cream or second-press coconut milk, blend both the first- and second-press milks together. Coconut milk can be prepared in advance and can be frozen for up to 6 months.

PREPARING PRAWNS

1 Hold the body of the prawn firmly, squeeze and pull off the head. Peel away the shell and legs from the body, then holding the body squeeze off the tail. Reserve the shell and head if using in a recipe – they are also great to flavour a stock.

2 To devein the prawn, hold it so the back of the prawn is slightly curved. Using a small knife, make a shallow incision along the back. Use a cocktail stick to remove the black vein.

3 If the prawns are to be used whole, make a few incisions vertically along the belly. This will prevent it from curling during cooking.

4 Rinse the prawns in running cold water and drain. Transfer the prawns to a deep bowl, add 1 tablespoon sea salt and use your hands to lightly massage the salt into the prawns. The use of salt at this stage is to give the prawns a springy texture. Rinse the prawns under running cold water, drain and pat dry with kitchen paper.

PREPARING SQUID

1 Place the squid on a chopping board and spread the tentacles out on the board. Cut off and discard the two longest tentacles.

2 Take the head in one hand and the body in the other and gently pull the head away from the body. It will take the intestines with it. Cut just in front of the eyes and remove and discard the eyes and intestines.

3 Next, pull out and discard the inedible beak from the base of the tentacles and the transparent silver quill found inside the body.

4 Finally, pull off the two fins on either side of the body and pull away the spotty skin from both the body and the fins. Discard the fins and use the tentacles, if you like. Thoroughly rinse the pieces of squid, inside and out, under running cold water, then pat dry with kitchen paper.

5 Squid can be cut into rings or scored with a diamond pattern. To do this, cut open the body by sliding a sharp, flexible knife into the opening of the body and along its entire length. Flatten the body out on a chopping board, inner surface facing up. Position your knife at 90° to the surface, then make very shallow diagonal crisscross cuts in the flesh. By scoring the squid on the inside surface, it will curl with the inside facing out when cooked. Cut the body into pieces according to the recipe instructions.

PREPARING BEEF TO BE THINLY SLICED

1 Rinse the beef under running cold water and pat dry with kitchen paper. Cover with cling film and freeze for about 25 minutes, so that the beef is firm to the touch but not frozen solid.

2 Remove the beef from the freezer, unwrap the cling film and place the beef on a chopping board. Using a sharp knife, cut the beef against the grain into 3mm/⅛in slices, or even thinner if possible.

REHYDRATING DRIED MUSHROOMS

1 Put the dried mushrooms in a bowl, pour over boiling water and soak for 20–25 minutes until soft. Drain off the liquid, straining the liquid into a clean bowl, if using, and squeeze off any excess liquid. Trim off the stems.

ROASTED SHRIMP PASTE

1 Put the recipe quantity of shrimp paste in the middle of a square piece of foil and break it into pieces with a spoon. Fold in the edges to form a small package and roast in a preheated oven at 200°C/400°F/Gas 6 for about 5 minutes. Remove and leave to one side to cool. The roasted shrimp will smell aromatic and be a darker-coloured dry powder.

SKINNING TOMATOES

1 Score the base of the tomato, put in a bowl and cover with boiling water. Leave to stand until the skin starts to curl, then drain off the water and fill the bowl with cold water. Leave to cool a little and remove the skin.

TAMARIND WATER

1 Put 50g/1¾oz tamarind pulp and 80ml/2½fl oz/⅓ cup boiling water in a small bowl. Soak for 30 minutes until soft. Use the back of a spoon to break the pulp into a pliable form, then strain through a fine sieve set over a bowl. Discard the solids.

TOASTED DRIED ANCHOVIES

1 Remove the heads and guts from the dried anchovies, then rinse under running cold water, drain and pat dry with kitchen paper.

2 Heat 1 teaspoon vegetable oil in a frying pan over a medium heat. Add the anchovies and toast until they turn golden brown.

glossary

BEAN CURD SHEET This is made from the layer of film that forms on the surface of soya milk when it is made. The film is collected and dried to become a translucent sheet.

BLACK BEAN PASTE Made from fermented and salted soya beans and with a pungent smell and bitter-sweet taste, black bean paste is often used in stir-fries.

BONITO FLAKES, DRIED Known as katsuobushi in Japanese, bonito flakes are dried, fermented and smoked skipjack tuna shavings that are commonly used in making dashi stock and miso soup.

CHILLI BEAN PASTE Also known as dou ban jiang in Chinese Mandarin. Chilli bean paste is made of chilli pepper, fermented soya beans, fermented broad beans and a mix of spices. It tastes both slightly spicy and salty at the same time.

CHINESE BLACK RICE VINEGAR Sometimes called Chinkiang vinegar, after the place it is produced, this vinegar tastes very similar to balsamic vinegar. It is often used in dipping sauces and in stir-fries.

CHINESE FIVE-SPICE This is a mix of five spices including black peppercorns, cloves, cinnamon, fennel seed and star anise. It is used in braised dishes and also to marinate meat. Ready-ground powder is readily available in the supermarket.

DAIKON Also known as Chinese radish or mooli in India, daikon is shaped like a very long carrot and has a mild flavour. It is often used in Japanese stews and as a pickle.

DRIED ANCHOVIES These are the small, salt-water fish that have been dried. Dried anchovies are often used in Korean cuisine as a stock base and are commonly use in sambal dishes in Malaysia and Indonesia. Most of the time, however, they are fried to give a crispy texture and added to salads or fried rice.

GALANGAL It is a rhizome from the ginger family. It has a pale yellow and pinkish skin and citrusy flavour. Galangal is normally used in curry pastes or to infuse stock.

GLUTINOUS RICE It is a type of short-grain rice that becomes very sticky once cooked. It is sometimes called sticky rice, and is normally soaked before steaming.

GLUTINOUS RICE FLOUR A highly absorbent flour made from glutinous rice. Often used to make Asian desserts, it becomes sticky, rubbery and chewy in texture.

HOISIN SAUCE It is commonly used as a condiment. It has a thick and sticky texture with a brown colour. It is made from soya beans, vinegar, sugar and other spices. It is a popular ingredient in marainades as it has sweet and garlicky taste.

JERUSALEM ARTICHOKES Not related to the artichoke family, Jerusalem artichoke is a root vegetable that looks very like ginger. It has a sweet and nutty flavour and a crisp and crunchy texture, and can be eaten either raw or cooked.

JICAMA Also known as yam bean, jicama is a root vegetable that is commonly used in Southeast Asian and Central American cooking. It has a similar shape to the white round radish but it is bigger. Jicama has a crunchy texture and can be eaten raw and cooked. Substitutes are Jerusalem artichokes and water chestnuts.

KOMBU, DRIED An edible kelp that is widely used in Japanese cooking and, in the dried form, is one of the main ingredients in dashi. It is also sold pickled.

KOREAN RED PEPPER POWDER Called kochukara in Korea, this is a powder form of Korean dried red pepper. Korean red pepper is another variety of red chilli that is sun-dried. It is used in many Korean dishes such as kimchi and bulgogi.

KOREAN HOT PEPPER PASTE Called gochujang in Korea, this paste is salty, spicy and pungent. It is made from Korean dried red pepper, fermented soya beans and other spices. It is normally used as a condiment, marinade or seasoning. It is almost equivalent to Chilli Bean Paste.

LOTUS LEAVES From the lotus plant and used dried, the lotus leaf is a bright green colour and big. It is most often used to cook sticky rice in to give it a more earthy and smoky flavour as well as to keep the ingredients moist.

MIRIN A Japanese sweet rice wine with a low alcohol content. It has a strong flavour, is very sweet and is often used instead of sugar.

NORI A dried sheet of seaweed, which is used to make sushi and sometimes as a garnish. It is slightly salty in flavour and has a crispy texture.

PALM SUGAR Widely used in Asian cooking, palm sugar is obtained from the sugary sap of certain palm trees. It usually comes in blocks, which you can chop or slice up, but is also found in granular and liquid form. If not available, replace with soft light brown sugar.

PANDAN LEAVES Also known as screwpine leaves, pandan leaves are green, thin, long and pointed, and are used as a flavouring in savoury dishes and a colouring in desserts. When used as a flavouring in stocks or rice, they are normally tied into a knot for easy removal. Alternatively, they are snipped into pieces and then blended into a paste. The juice is then squeezed out and used. Pandan essence can be found at Asian supermarkets and is mostly used in making desserts.

SAGO PEARLS Sago is extracted from the pith of sago palm stems. They are very tiny and white. Sago pearls are commonly used in Southeast Asia in desserts, and when cooked turn translucent.

SAKE A popular alcoholic drink in Japan, sake is made from fermented rice. Because 'drinking' sake is quite expensive to be used in cooking, there is a cheaper cooking variety that can be found in Asian supermarkets.

SHOYU It is the Japanese version of light soy sauce, which has a richer and stronger flavour compared to Chinese light soy sauce. It is great in stir-fries, marinades or as condiment.

SHRIMP PASTE Shrimp paste is widely used in Southeast Asian cooking, normally comes in a block and is made from fermented shrimp that is dried in the sun. It is known as belacan in Malay, terasi in Indonesian, kapi in Thai and khmer mam ruoc in Vietnamese. Uncooked shrimp paste is a bit sticky and has a pungent and strong fishy smell. Because of this, it is not advisable to toast shrimp paste in a pan in your kitchen, but to roast it in the oven instead (*see page 217*).

SICHUAN PEPPERCORNS They are reddish-brown in colour, have a very unique and strong flavour and are normally toasted before use in order to bring out the aroma.

TAMARIND PEEL This is sun-dried slices of the small, round, sour-tasting asam gelugor fruit grown on a tree native to Malaysia. It is also known as asam keping and not related to the tamarind fruit. Tamarind peel is mostly used in fish-based curries in Malaysia and Singapore.

TAMARIND PULP This is the sticky pulp taken from the inside of the tamarind pod. It is dark brown in colour and is normally sold in a block. The pulp needs to be soaked in warm water for about 30 minutes before use to make tamarind water (*see page 217*).

THAI BASIL The Thai basil leaf is long and pointed and the stem is purple. It has a much stronger and more pungent flavour than sweet basil and is normally used in salads, stir-fries and curry dishes.

VIETNAMESE CORIANDER LEAVES This is the most common name for polygonum leaves and is also known as Vietnamese mint as well as laksa leaves in Indonesia and daun kesom in Malaysia and Singapore. They are normally used to infuse soup stock.

WAKAME Wakame is a long, deep green seaweed that usually comes in a dried form. A popular ingredient in Japanese cuisine, it is commonly used in salads or added to miso soup. Dried wakame has to be rehydrated in water before it can be used.

WATER CHESTNUTS An aquatic vegetable that is small and round. They can be eaten raw or cooked and the flesh has a crunchy texture.

WATER SPINACH Known as ong choi in China, this is a semi-aquatic vegetable with long, pointed leaves and a long, hollow stem. The texture is crunchy and it is normally used in stir-fries and soup dishes.

WASABI Also known as Japanese horseradish, wasabi has a very strong and fiery flavour. Once eaten, it stimulates the nasal passage, unlike chilli, which produces a hot sensation on the tongue. Wasabi is most commonly used as a condiment for sushi.

INDEX

AUTHOR ACKNOWLEDGEMENTS

Thank you to…
Arnaud, for being so very patient and supportive throughout the period that this book was being written. It wouldn't have been the same without your feedback when I was testing the recipes.
Mum and Dad, for bringing me into this world and for all your guidance and advice all these years.
My sister, for all of your great effort in helping me to test and re-test the recipes. I wouldn't have been able to make it without your help.
My brother, for loving my food since you were little.
Nelly, for your support and testing some of the recipes. You have inspired me!
Azma, for being a great friend and for helping with the recipe testing. You put a smile on my face when you said, 'It's very delicious!'
Kristin, I finally managed to get you to cook and I hope this is just the beginning of the journey.
Grace, for your patience, guidance and support. It has been a great pleasure to know you. Thank you for giving me this amazing opportunity to author this book!
Camilla, for your great work in editing this book. Your words of encouragement have given me even more confidence in and enthusiasm for writing!
The loyal readers of my blog, My Cooking Hut, for your readership, support and words of encouragement.

Thank you, Lord, for being my strength and guidance.

TEXTILE PHOTO CREDITS